DIETER BROCK
The Birmingham Rifle
Robert Allan Young

ISBN 978-1-7750340-2-5
1.   Biography & Autobiography
2.   Sports

Special Thanks

There are so many people who helped inspire and create this book. First and foremost, thank you Cathy Garski for sending me that original message. I have to give a heartfelt thanks to people like Trevor Kennard, Snapper Lancaster, Tom Cudney, John Bonk, Harry Knight, J.C. Smith, Ray Jauch, Leo Ezerins, Peter Young, Kathy K.K. Kennedy, Chris Walby, James West, Greg Mackling, Brenda Bourns, Dave Petrishen, Jason Johnson and Paul Bennett.

I can't forget Lyle and Heidi Bauer, who started this incredible journey and after publishing three other books, made me an overnight success.

A huge thank you to my three sons; Adam, Kevin and Marc and I can't forget Joel, Jessica and Dorothy as well.

And of course there's, Lisa, my reader, my best friend and my love. This wouldn't have come together without your unwavering support.

Thank you Dieter and Jaime for allowing me to tell an amazing story and for putting your trust and confidence in me through this whole project.

To A Mouse (English Translation)

Small, crafty, cowering, timorous little beast,
Oh, what a panic is in your breast!
You need not start away so hasty
With your hurrying scamper
I would be loath to run and chase you,
With murdering plough-staff.

I'm truly sorry man's dominion
Has broken Nature's social union,
And justifies that ill opinion
Which makes you startle
At me, your poor, earth born companion
And fellow mortal!

I doubt not, sometimes, but you may steal;
What then? Poor little beast, you must live!
An odd ear in twenty-four sheaves
Is a small request;
I will get a blessing with what is left,
And never miss it.

Your small house, too, in ruin!
Its feeble walls the winds are scattering!
And nothing now, to build a new one,
Of coarse grass green!
And bleak December's winds coming,
Both bitter and piercing!

You saw the fields laid bare and wasted,
And weary winter coming fast,
And cozy here, beneath the blast,
You thought to dwell,
Till crash! the cruel plough passed
Out through your cell.

That small bit heap of leaves and stubble,
Has cost you many a weary nibble!
Now you are turned out, for all your trouble,
Without house or holding,
To endure the winter's sleety dribble,
And hoar-frost cold.

But little Mouse, you are not alone,
In proving foresight may be vain:
The best laid schemes of mice and men
Go often askew,
And leave us nothing but grief and pain,
For promised joy!

Still you are blessed, compared with me!
The present only touches you:
But oh! I backward cast my eye,
On prospects dreary!
And forward, though I cannot see,
I guess and fear!

Robert Burns

Table of Contents

Chapter One

"He pissed me off! How could he have done that?"

Greg Mackling is one of the co-hosts of Corus Radio's, CJOB Morning Show in Winnipeg. In a casual, off-air conversation, he recalled the start of the Winnipeg Blue Bombers' 1983 season. "I think I was in the 7th or 8th grade when all that happened," he said.

"My family used to live in Winnipeg's West End. It was so close to the Stadium I could see the lights from my bedroom window and we could hear the crowd during the games. Of course I was a fan of the Blue and Gold and like any kid, I wanted to go to every game."

In their previous season, Winnipeg Blue Bombers had finished in 2nd place in the West Division with an impressive 11–5 record. Unfortunately, they had lost 24-21 to the Edmonton Eskimos in the West Final but with new head coach, Cal Murphy bringing in a new philosophy and system to the club, everyone thought 1983 was going to be their year.

"I took a paper route in the neighbourhood so I could earn enough money to buy my own tickets to the games that year. I spent the winter delivering papers in -20 degree weather just so I could see my Bombers win. I was so excited. Bob Cameron even lived on my route," Mackling said.

"And then, before the season even starts, he decides he's too good for Winnipeg. He hates it here and he's not coming back."

The focus of Mackling's anger was Winnipeg Blue Bombers' starting quarterback, Dieter Brock. After nine seasons leading the team, the thirty-one year old quarterback from Alabama announced his retirement.

Ralph Dieter Brock was born on February 12, 1951 in Gadsden, Alabama, 60 miles northeast of Birmingham. He had attended Auburn University and Jacksonville State University. He played for both schools, posting numerous records and even received a Hall of Fame induction at Jacksonville State.

In 1974, Ralph Brock signed a one-year contract with the Canadian Football League's Winnipeg Blue Bombers where he would start his professional football career as the back-up quarterback to seasoned veteran, Don Jonas.

In 1975, the team traded away their aging quarterback to the Hamilton Tiger-Cats for a much younger Chuck Ealey.

Brock's future with the Blue Bombers was still in question. General Manager Earl Lunsford and Coach Bud Riley were still searching for the right pieces to complete their offence and brought in several young quarterbacks to compete for the back-up position.

Midway through the season Brock would outperform Ealey and become the team's starter, resulting in Ealey being dealt to the Toronto Argonauts. The Winnipeg Blue Bombers were now Dieter Brock's team.

The late Winnipeg newspaperman, Jack Matheson once wrote, "Ralph Dieter Brock could throw holes in the wind." Impressed with the strength in his arm earned Brock the nickname, "The Birmingham Rifle" from Matheson.

Eventually, Brock became the only Winnipeg Blue Bombers' player to win back-to-back Canadian Football League Most Outstanding Player awards for the 1980 and 1981 CFL seasons.

In 1981, Ralph Dieter Brock broke Sam Etcheverry's 1956 record of 4,723 passing yards with 4,796 yards. In his career, he had complied 34,830 yards in the air on 4,535 pass attempts with 2,602 completions.

He threw 210 touchdown passes and had a 57% completion ratio. On October 3, 1981 Brock completed 41 passes, 16 of them consecutively, and finished the day with an outstanding 87% passing percentage. He was the CFL's passing leader in 1978, 1980, 1981 and 1984. Dieter Brock still holds the Winnipeg Blue Bombers record for career passing yards with 29,623.

But on April 29, 1983, Dieter Brock announced his retirement. After nine seasons as the quarterback for the Winnipeg Blue Bombers, Winnipeg's love affair with Dieter Brock was about to end on a sour note. With three years plus an option remaining on his $1.1 million dollar contract, he had decided to stay home in Birmingham, Alabama.

"He upset the entire city of Winnipeg," said Dave Petrishen, The Sports Doctor. "But it's still hard to fully understand that whole situation. On one hand, it didn't make sense. If you really think about it, we all have friends who leave one company or organization for better opportunities or money at another. And we're happy for them. But with Dieter, that situation was completely different."

And it's true. As Brock's situation with the Blue Bombers unfolded in the press, Serge Savard, the Winnipeg Jets all-star, legendary defencemen had also announced his early retirement to go back to the Montreal Canadiens. But he received praises and well wishes from the team and the city.

South of the border, the Baltimore Ravens had chosen a young John Elway as their first selection in the 1983 NFL Draft despite his numerous public announcements that he would not be reporting to the team. Elway was going to hold out for a better team and a better offer. But he hadn't received the negative flogging from the press or the public that was being unleashed on Brock.

Let's face it, we all have heroes or people we look up to and admire. It is perfectly normal. Sometimes, that person is a real world influence, such as a political leader or activist. But more often than not, our focus is on a celebrity and that celebrity is often an athlete.

We look up to these figures. We follow their every move and hang on every comment. We buy their jerseys and proudly wear their numbers as often as we can. They motivate and inspire us, up until that moment when they let us down.

Suddenly, when our heroes falter, either on or off the field, we do our best to distance ourselves from them. We lash out. We become resentful and angry, not wanting to associate with the disappointment they have created in our lives. The deeper our investment in our hero's accomplishments and the more we define ourselves through their achievements, the more resentment we hold inside when they let us down.

But, just in case you haven't figured it out yet, humans are flawed. They make mistakes. They say things in ignorance, anger and disappointment just like you and I have done and probably will continue to do.

It hurts when our heroes let us down and disappoint us. It can be hard to forgive a hero's personal shortcomings because most of the time we have been in their same situation. Maybe not in the same public eye or to the same degree, but we have all messed up at some point in our lives. Yes, we can always choose our heroes, but can we choose to forgive?

After months of controversy, the Winnipeg Blue Bombers eventually traded Dieter Brock to the Hamilton Tiger-Cats for quarterback Tom Clements. That trade eventually led to an exciting Grey Cup game in 1984 as the Tiger-Cats and Blue Bombers went head to head against each other. Brock's Ticats would lose the game to Clements's Blue Bombers 47-17.

Dieter Brock left the Canadian Football League after the 1984 season and set his sights on the National Football League the following year. He was invited to try out for the Buffalo Bills, Green Bay Packers, Cleveland Browns and the Los Angeles Rams.

In what would be his only season playing in the National Football League, Brock chose to sign with the Los Angeles Rams as a 33-year-old rookie. He led the team to a division title, the number two seed in the NFC playoffs, and set team rookie records for passing yards, touchdown passes, and passer rating.

His final game was the 1985 NFC Championship Game against the Chicago Bears, where he managed just 66 yards passing and lost a fumble that Bear's Wilber Marshall returned for a touchdown to close out the scoring in a 24-0 game.

"I was actually excited when he signed with the Rams," said Mackling. "I really followed his career closely after he left the CFL. I mean, he started here. It all started here."

"I remember when all that was going on," said local Winnipeg author, Carlene Rummery. "He had been my hero. I was twelve and I was pissed! I was mad at the Bombers, too. I didn't know who to blame at the time."

Carlene's husband Randy, who she refers to as a Brock Nerd, echoes his wife's sentiments. "I can recall Brock making a lot of negative comments about Winnipeg, the main one being something like "Winnipeg is so boring, there's nothing to do here but go to the zoo" or something along those lines," said Randy.

"I was thirteen or fourteen at the time and had very little understanding of what holdouts or negotiations were all about," said Randy. "By the time he was in Hamilton, I remember he was widely disliked in Winnipeg, and it seemed everyone had a Brock Busters t-shirt. I remember how loud the cheers were whenever he got sacked, especially in the '84 Grey Cup."

We know there were telephone calls and meetings between the Blue Bombers and Brock. We know the Blue Bombers' general manager flew down to Birmingham to personally meet with Brock and his agent, Gil Scott. We also know that Brock returned to Winnipeg only to pack his bags and leave again.

But after more than thirty years, we still don't understand what really happened. We don't know who was responsible or who to blame. All we know is the disappointment that fell over our entire city. We don't know the private conversations or the thought process behind the decisions that were made. We don't know the motivations, the intentions or even the hopes and dreams of those involved.

Our entire world can shift when a hero fails us. It can become more negative and less hopeful. But as time passes and we grow older, as we learn and experience more things in life, we discover that our definition of a hero changes. The heroes we had yesterday are no longer important because they no longer serve the same purpose. Did they disappear or have we been forced to face the reality of growing up and understanding?

And how do you live in a world where our heroes fail us? Some say you should never meet your heroes, but I think we should. I believe if we do we'll discover that most are more like us than we ever would have imagined and it allows us to move from knowing to understanding.

When it comes to our heroes, we only know what we've been told to know, and in the case of Ralph Dieter Brock, "The Birmingham Rifle," knowing does not mean understanding.

Chapter Two

In July 2017, Bruce Arians, the former head coach of the Arizona Cardinals released a book titled 'The Quarterback Whisperer.' Coach Arians had a long, winding journey through the world of football, having coached for thirty-seven years between the college and professional ranks before becoming a head coach in the NFL in 2013. The former Cardinals' coach is well known for his guidance and teaching of Peyton Manning, Ben Roethlisberger, Andrew Luck and Carson Palmer.

In his book, he defines what it takes to become a great quarterback with a few distinct characteristics: heart, grit, intelligence, accuracy and athleticism.

In summary, Coach Arians details the characteristics as;

Heart: the ability to perform through pain and earn the respect of the entire roster,

Grit: The ability to handle success and failure equally,

Intelligence: The ability to process information from film and practice into a game situation and make the right decisions in a split second or two,

Accuracy: The ability to throw the ball with accuracy to all parts of the field,

Athleticism: To be able to move in the pocket and extend plays.

The quarterback position is unique, not just in football, but in all sports. It requires a physical skill set unlike any other, but most of all, it requires a specific disposition which is rare in occurrence and difficult to quantify. Don Klosterman was one of professional football's most accomplished executives. He built teams in three different leagues after a serious accident ended his playing career as a quarterback. The former Baltimore Colts and Los Angeles Rams General Manager may have put it best when he said, "Do not evaluate a quarterback the way you evaluate the other twenty-one positions. They're playing a different sport. With a quarterback, it's the things you can't put down on paper that make all the difference."

When any player makes it as a professional quarterback, it's clear that they possess the physical attributes to make it in the professional arena. However, with the quarterback position, it's the intangibles that make the greatest difference and will separate the elite players from average ones. The greatest quarterbacks to ever play the game have not necessarily been the most talented – it's their character that sets them apart and that has to come from somewhere.

"I played in an era in the CFL where there were six Hall of Fame quarterbacks playing," said Brock. "Ron Lancaster, Tom Wilkinson, Tom Clements, Condredge Holloway, Warren Moon and myself. Matt Dunigan was a backup to Warren Moon and became a starter in my last year in the CFL. And he certainly was a Hall of Fame quarterback. But in my opinion, the most talented overall was Warren Moon."

"And by most talented I mean quarterbacks who had great arms, powerful accurate passers who were fun and exciting to watch and could play in any system. "I didn't play against all these guys obviously, but these are the ones that came to mind when I think of talented quarterbacks."

"The ones that I think were and are the most talented other than Moon were Joe Namath, John Elway, Brett Favre, Dan Marino, Terry Bradshaw, Sonny Jurgensen, Matt Dunigan, Aaron Rodgers," he said. "But who I consider maybe the most talented and he's not even in the Hall of Fame is Bert Jones who played at LSU and later with the Baltimore Colts in the NFL."

"I still think you have to judge quarterbacks in the era that they played in because the game has changed over the years. The game was different when I was growing up."

"My first recollection growing up was almost always following my older brother, Billy Joe everywhere. He was sixteen months older than me," said Brock. "We were just kids running wild all over the place. We had rock-throwing and BB gun battles against neighbourhood kids. We hopped on moving trains.

"We did all kinds of crazy things," he said. "When I think back, we really were lucky that we didn't get hurt any worse than the few minor injuries. That's probably why Billy Joe earned the nickname 'Wild Bill' later on."

"I really didn't know much about my Dad's younger years," Brock continued. "He joined the Merchant Marines when he was fourteen or fifteen. He actually had to lie about his age at the time in order to sign up."

As a member of the U.S. Merchant Marines, young William Brock and crew were primarily responsible for transporting cargo and passengers during peacetime. But in times of war, they could be an auxiliary to the U. S. Navy and used to deliver military personnel and material into war zones.

Merchant mariners were the supply line that provided virtually everything Allied armies needed in order to survive and fight on foreign battlefields. The seamen had no military standing or government benefits, but they possessed an unusual variety of courage and gave their lives for their country as valiantly as those in the armed forces did.

"After World War II, my father starting working as a Military Policeman in Stuttgart, Germany," said Brock. "That's where he met my mother, Emmy Marie."

"After the war, they married and moved back to the States to Alabama. He eventually got a job as a welder with U.S. Steel."

William and Emmy Marie Brock settled in Gadsden, Alabama, sixty miles northeast of Birmingham.

"I was born in Gadsden, but we only lived there a year or so before moving to Talladega, Alabama. We eventually moved to Birmingham when I was five."

In the early 1960s, Birmingham, Alabama was one of the most racially divided cities in the United States.

African-American citizens faced legal, educational and economic disparities and violent retribution when they attempted to draw attention to their problems. Martin Luther King Jr. had called it the most segregated city in the country.

The protests in Birmingham initially began in 1963 with a boycott meant to pressure business leaders to open employment to people of all races, and end segregation in public facilities, restaurants, schools, and stores. When local business and governmental leaders resisted the boycott, the Southern Christian Leadership Conference agreed to assist. The SCLC`s intention was to bring attention to the integration efforts of African Americans in Birmingham.

"I remember the racial tensions. I knew a little bit about what was going on through the newspaper and on TV, even though we only had three television channels," said Brock.

"My high school, Jones Valley, was an all-white school I think until 1967. We did have a few black students come in around my junior year and we had one or two black players on the football team. We had one really outstanding black player named was Michael Leonard on the basketball team. He was a six foot four center and quite a good player. But we were kids. From what I remember we all got along great. There weren't any problems at school."

But outside the classrooms and off the sports fields and playgrounds, things were quite different. Led by Martin Luther King Jr. and others, their campaign of nonviolent, direct action resulted in widely publicized confrontations and demonstrations on the streets of Birmingham. The movement eventually led the municipal government to change the city's discrimination laws, but unfortunately, laws don't necessarily change the hearts, thoughts and behaviors of all.

"It didn't have an effect on me too much other than I knew what was happening wasn't right. I know this was the way some whites grew up, believing that blacks were second-class citizens or sometimes not even citizens at all back in the 50s and 60s. It's the way they were taught by their parents and their grandparents," said Brock.

"Thank God I was young enough in the 1950s that I didn't understand it all that well. I didn't know exactly what was going on," he continued. "But by the middle to late 60s, I knew how wrong all that was, all those terrible things that were done. I just couldn't believe people could think this way and do those things to another group of people."

"I have to honestly say that my dad was probably part of that group. I think he thought along with a lot of other people at the time that blacks should be kept in segregation."

"Despite that, Dad was a good provider," said Brock. "I don't think we lacked for the things we needed growing up. But I do remember, with his military background he was strict."

"We would get a whipping with a belt occasionally," he recalled. "And there were a lot of times when he didn't want other kids coming over to the house, but there were always kids around the neighborhood. It's what we did. Because Dad was so strict my brother, Billy Joe gave him the nickname the 'Warden,' and all our friends would refer to him as that too."

"He worked different shifts all the time so he was in and out of the house at different times," says Brock. "When we had the chance, we did things like going on beach vacations to Florida every year and out to dinner at times. We went to the fair a lot, too."

"We had a lot of work around the house that we had to do like washing dishes, cutting grass, waxing the hardwood floors and chores like that. I guess that's all just normal stuff."

"But we got into trouble a lot. I think I was six when we hopped on a moving train that went from North Birmingham where we lived to downtown. We had to get someone to call our parents to come and pick us up. They weren't too happy."

"We moved to a suburb of Birmingham called Green Acres when I was seven. It was about two blocks from

Green Acres Elementary School. It was close enough that on my lunch break, I would ride home on my bicycle with some friends. That's what we could do back in those days. My parents were working so I would be going home by myself to eat lunch or go hang out with some friends to the local Zippy Mart."

Like most boys that age, Brock had his heroes and one in particular that became his focus. But when you chose someone that flies through the air at death defying speeds, the difference between fantasy and reality can be a bit dangerous. "I think I was eight or nine when I decided I wanted to be Evil Knievel," he recalls. "I decided to set up a jump in the driveway at lunchtime."

"But I got a little nervous as I got close to the ramp and slowed down too much just as I hit it. Instead of flying through the air, I dropped head first into the ground and knocked myself out. When I woke up, I couldn't remember where I was."

"Somehow I rode back to school on my bike with a friend. But instead of going to class, we had to go to the principal's office because I couldn't remember where I was. They had no choice but to call my parents to come get me and take me to the doctor."

"When we got to the doctor's office, I started getting my memory back, but I wasn't going to tell my Dad that, because I knew he would kill me."

The rough, risk- taking play that so many young boys are fond of, which some experts say begins around age three and peaks between ages eight and ten, often turns competitive. Some boys are just hard-wired to form social groups in which they start to compete against other boys.

"I think the thing that saved me from getting killed was that we all really got into sports," said Brock.

Despite his notoriety with a football, it was a baseball that first put the sports bug in Brock. "We played all the time after school," he said. "We were always forming teams with other kids and played neighbourhood baseball games all the time."

"I remember one of the things that I did that helped me develop my arm was that I would be the pitcher and my brother would be the batter," said Brock. "I used to pretend that I was the fastest pitcher in world and we would play a full nine inning game just to see how many strikeouts I could get."

"We used a rubber ball and I would throw it against the house which was made of brick and if he missed hitting it, it would just bounce right back to me. When I think back, it was a good time to grow up because everything seemed so simple back then."

The simple Southern life started to turn competitive at a young age for Brock. "I was just a kid who wanted to throw the ball harder and faster than anyone else."

"I started playing Little League baseball at nine years old. I was still following my brother who was quite a good baseball player. I would have to ride my bike three miles to practice, then ride all the way back home in the dark."

"Once I started Little League, I started collecting baseball and football cards. It wasn't long before I knew the stats of every great ball player. I could tell you Babe Ruth's lifetime batting average. Ted Williams, Ty Cobb, I knew them all. I just loved the game. I knew the lineups of just about every major league baseball team at that time."

"Billy Joe was the starting right fielder of the Central Park Dixie Youth Boys World Series team that won the championship back in 1962. Central Park Little League was where we played growing up. It was the ten through twelve year old age group. He was twelve and I was on the same team as an eleven year old, but I didn't make the All-Star team. I had improved a lot from a ten year old where I couldn't even catch a fly ball or get a hit."

Pat Patrick, a long-time friend of the Brock brothers remembers the early days in Birmingham. "On the west side in the late 50's and early 60's, there were a number of communities with numerous elementary schools and high schools as well as parks that had football and baseball fields."

"At that time, football at the college level, for the longest time had been "King" in Alabama," said Patrick. "But at the park level, the interest in youth league baseball greatly surpassed youth football. Remember, this was the days of Mickey Mantle, Yogi Berra, Hank Aaron and Willie Mays."

"In the first ten years of its existence, the Major League 11 and 12 year old World Championships were won by either Central Park or Midfield. Dieter and his brother both played for Central Park, but Wild Bill Brock was definitely one of the standouts for the champions."

Even when, as an eleven year old, Dieter had made the twelve year old All-Star team, he was still living in the shadow of older brother.

"I remember competing against both of them," Patrick continued. "It was never at the high school level, but at the park level. That was really where you could take chances and see some outstanding baseball. Dieter played third base because of his strong right arm. And, even in junior high he could throw the ball with great velocity."

"The only organized sport that I played was baseball until I got the high school," said Brock. "I did go out for football for one day at the Central Park 80 lb Football League, but that didn't work out the way I thought. I wanted to play quarterback, but all they did was use me to do drills."

"I went to Jones Valley High School as freshman in 1965," said Brock. "Jones Valley was a 4A School which meant it was one of the larger schools in the state. I went out for the freshman football team or B Team as it was called."

"I think deep down, even back then, I wanted to play quarterback," said Brock. "But I was too shy and afraid to say anything, so I let them just put me wherever they wanted. Eventually the coach put me in as a defensive back and I was terrible."

After excelling in baseball and the neighbourhood pick-up games, the idea of not performing to what he felt was his best, hit Brock hard. "I had never played organized football before. I didn't know what the hell I was doing."

In the southern United States, high school football ranks almost as high as religion. It's an environment where teen-age star football players are treated 'like privileged children of royalty.' Performance on the field can mean everything to a young player.

"Dieter and I were new teammates at Jones Valley High School as freshmen," recalls Patrick. "As a freshman I had a pretty good year, but not Dieter. He didn't get to play a single down."

"Even during the last game of the season," said Dieter. "The coach had told us that every player was going to play. We got deep into the fourth quarter and he still hadn't been put in the game."

It can damage a young ego to be the only one sitting alone on the bench, especially when there are special spectators in the stands watching. "My parents were at that game. They came to see me play, but I hid at the far end of the bench. It was embarrassing!"

As the clock clicked towards the end of the fourth quarter, Brock's aspirations sunk. "I didn't want to go in that late in the game. I was the only player on the entire team that didn't play."

Despite his dismal experience with football, and after the hurt had subsided, Brock was still determined.

"After that football season, I went out for basketball and baseball and I was pretty good at both," said Brock. "Basketball was really my favorite sport. I was the starting guard as a sophomore on the varsity basketball team. I ended up being the leading scorer on the basketball team all three years averaging close to 20 points a game. I once hit 93 out of 100 free throws with 53 in a row."

His high school performance was starting to gain some attention around the state, but it wasn't for football or even baseball. "I was getting interest from colleges about playing basketball."

"I felt bad for him," said Patrick. "He decided he was going to quit football and not play his sophomore year."

"My best friend in high school was Johnny Colburn," recalls Brock. "When I wasn't playing sports, I hung around with Johnny and Wild and a few other friends. We weren't the most innocent group of guys, that's for sure. We did a lot of crazy things."

"One time we went to watch Joe Namath and the New York Jets play the Baltimore Colts in an exhibition game at Legion Field in Birmingham," said Brock. "There was Johnny, Wild Bill, Mike Walls, whose nickname was "Fats," and I. Hey, everyone had a nickname back then."

"Well, we were at the game and started talking about grabbing one of the footballs off the field and taking off with it," said Brock. Their opportunity presented itself when the legend, Joe Namath threw a long incomplete pass that went into the end zone. "Fats jumped the fence and grabbed the ball. Then he tossed it over to Johnny, who threw it over to me. Wild Bill ran outside the stadium so that I could throw it to him and he would take off with it."

"Well, the cops started running all over the stadium trying to get the football back," laughed Brock. "Fans in the stadium were up on their feet watching and cheering us on. It must have been quite the spectacle because the next day's newspaper reported that we were one of the most exciting things they had seen during the game."

"Of course we got caught," said Brock "But we weren't arrested. They just kicked us out of the game and took the football back."

"Even back then, I just wanted to throw the ball," he said. "I just wanted to hang out with my friends and throw it. That's what I was good at."

His freshman year of football had been such a nightmare that initially he had no intention of ever returning to the field. But over time, his embarrassment subsided and his completive nature took over. "I was so terrible at football my freshman year that my brother Billy bet that I would never go out again," said Brock. "So, just to prove him wrong I went out for the team in my sophomore year."

"I was still a defensive back on the B team, but this time I knew more about what I was doing and was actually pretty good. I was a good tackler and I was able to defend pretty well."

Pat Patrick recalled the moment that everything shifted for Brock. "I think I was a favourite of our B Team Coach, the late Jimmy Currier," said Patrick. "I was short, but could throw the ball a little if we got outside the rush on roll-out passes. But about halfway through the season, we were not doing well."

"Coach Currier and I were walking out on the practice field while everyone else was warming up or goofing off," said Patrick. "Way down at the scoreboard end of the field, there were three or four guys dressed out in practice gear running pass patterns for fun. They didn't even have their head gear on."

"There was this guy, a right hander, running to his left and throwing the football against his body. Some of his passes were going 50 yards or more!"

"It was impressive. Coach Currier asked me, 'Who is that throwing the ball down there?' I replied, 'I think it is Brock, Coach.'"

"Coach just stood there quietly watching and then said to me, 'Well, get him down here and let's see what that kid can do.'"

After a few minutes, Ralph Brock showed Coach Currier what he could do with a football and was appointed the starting quarterback that afternoon. Pat Patrick was moved to running back.

As a quarterback, Brock was unfamiliar with the team's offence system and was lost when it came to calling the plays. The shift from defence to offence is not an easy task for the young player.

"Coach would send a play in to me," said Patrick. "I'd explain it to Dieter. He'd call it in the huddle and we'd run the play. We were successful the rest of our 10th grade year."

When the football season was over, Brock put his helmet and cleats away and headed back out to the basketball court where he continued to excel and make a name for himself.

"After the sophomore season of basketball was over, the Varsity football head coach, Bob Harris asked me if I was going to be his junior year quarterback the next season. He took notice of me when I became the starting quarterback for the B Team. He had seen my first game at quarterback where I threw three touchdown passes and looked pretty good."

"But he knew that Wild Bill was my brother. They had had a falling out at some point and Billy quit all sports," recalled Brock. "I think Coach Harris was concerned about me playing for him because of whatever happened. Of course at this time I was all in on playing all three sports; football, basketball and baseball. But, I told him yes without question!"

"I was brought up to the varsity team to finish the season, but not to play, just to dress out."

"The following year, Coach Harris had brought in a new offence called the Run and Shoot. He knew my throwing ability would be great in this offence. This was not the Mouse Davis Run and Shoot, this was the Tiger Ellison Run and Shoot and it was different."

The Tiger Ellison Run and Shoot system allows the quarterback more run options and play action passing. The Mouse Davis Run and Shoot is more of a passing offence.

"I was a pretty good runner back in those days; not fast, but shifty. Coach Harris put this offence in specifically for me and it worked. In my junior year we finished 8 -1- 1, third in the State just missing the championship. I was the All City quarterback, made All State completing almost 60% of my passes which at that time was unheard of, especially in high school football."

It would seem that Ralph Brock had found his lane and this is the part of the story where one would expect the all too common statement similar to all the other rags to riches sports tales, where the subject states "This was the point of my life where I knew sports could pull me towards a better life." But that's not his story. That's not who Dieter Brock was.

"All my athletic abilities seem to have come naturally, just from playing sports and throwing a ball all the time. We weren't into weightlifting or weight training at that time. I had really big hands and long arms and was just naturally strong."

"We used to climb trees a lot when I was growing up. We would pick the highest tree we could find and then see how high we could climb it," said Brock. He almost always out climbed the others.

Throughout his entire career, it's evident that Dieter Brock's "highest tree" philosophy was applied every time he stepped on to a field, in every situation, in every game and against every opponent. Point Dieter Brock to the "highest tree" in the forest and watch him climb higher than anyone else.

"I guess when you do something you love a lot, you just naturally become good at it. And back then, I was just a kid who loved to throw the ball."

Chapter Three

"Being perfect is not about that scoreboard out there. It's not about winning. It's about you and your relationship with yourself, your family and your friends. Being perfect is about being able to look your friends in the eye and know that you didn't let them down because you told them the truth. And that truth is you did everything you could. There wasn't one more thing you could've done. Can you live in that moment as best you can, with clear eyes, and love in your heart, with joy in your heart? If you can do that gentleman - you're perfect!"

Coach Gary Gaines, Friday Night Lights

The scene: the fall of 1967. The setting: late in the fourth quarter of the City High School Football Championship in Birmingham, Alabama. The situation: Banks High School 6, Jones Valley High 0.

Nothing compares to the tension and intensity of a championship football game between rival schools. Everything in life seems to be on the line for those sixty minutes.

"With five minutes left in the game and down 6-0, we drove 83 yards to tie the game 6 to 6. Our All-State fullback and linebacker, Jimmy Martin, who would sign a football scholarship to the University of Alabama, carried the ball most of the way with several runs. Facing a fourth and 5 from the 8-yard line, we called a roll out pass to the right and I hit Tommy Hopper, one of our slot backs with a pass that got us to the 2-yard line and a first down. From there

Jimmy Martin powered in for the tying touchdown with 28 seconds left in the game. Now all we needed was the extra point to win the game."

Brock ran back to sidelines to get instructions from Head Coach, Bob Harris for the final play of the game. The City Championship was on the line and the Jones Valley Brownies had just one shot left.

"As I was running to the sidelines, I noticed everyone was looking over at the goal post," said Brock. "I turned and saw some crazy guy had climbed up on the goal post after we scored the touchdown. The officials had to stop the game while the cops tried to get the guy down so we could kick the extra point."

"I remember walking by one the officials as he was saying 'I wonder who the hell that guy is,' said Brock. "But as soon as I looked up again, I knew who it was. It was Wild Bill!"

"Eventually they got him down. We kicked the extra point and won the game 7 to 6."

"I remember in that game, Banks High School had this guy, a senior running back and quarterback by the name of Johnny Musso. He was a beast on the field. He really did stand out in that game."

Johnny Musso graduated from Banks High School in 1968, a year before Brock and went on to play college football at the University of Alabama under the legendary Head Coach Bear Bryant. Musso was an All-American in 1971 at Alabama and led the Crimson Tide to an undefeated regular season and a berth in the Orange Bowl against top-ranked Nebraska.

Musso was a third round selection in the 1972 NFL draft, 62nd overall, by the Chicago Bears, but opted for a higher offer in the CFL instead. He played three seasons for the BC Lions (1972–1974), where he ran for 1029 yards in 1973 and was named a West Division All-Star.

"I didn't know it at the time but that game was watched by several college football coaches. Between the two teams, Jones Valley and Banks, there were nine players on each team that would eventually receive football scholarships," said Brock. "And I started receiving letters from colleges saying how interested they were in me."

A lot of young athletes go through high school living on the hope of an athletic scholarship. For some, it's the only way to further their education or athletic career. But to actually fulfill that goal to attend any college is extremely rare and difficult. The chances of receiving a Division 1 football scholarship are even more remote. In 1968, there were only about 115 Division 1 programs in the U.S. and with roughly one million high school players available, the odds of receiving an offer are less than one per cent.

"Yes, professional football was something that I really started to think about, so a scholarship would be a huge step for me," said Brock. "I was really excited when one of the schools that was interested in me was Alabama. Ever since Joe Namath came out of Alabama in 1965 and signed with the New York Jets, I wanted to be just like him."

Indeed, Division 1 schools were showing interest in the young junior quarterback. Georgia Tech and Auburn had also expressed interest in recruiting Brock to their programs.

"Out of the three, the University of Alabama was where I really wanted to go," said Brock. "Joe Namath had played there and of course because of Coach Bear Bryant. Everyone wanted to play under Coach Bryant."

Paul William "Bear" Bryant had taken over the University of Alabama football team in 1958. Prior to Bryant's arrival, Alabama had won just four games in their last three years. The Crimson Tide went 5–4–1 in Bryant's first season. The following year, 1959, Alabama beat Auburn and appeared in the inaugural Liberty Bowl game, the first time either had happened in six years.

In 1961, under his leadership and with quarterback Pat Trammell and football greats, Lee Roy Jordan and Billy Neighbors, Alabama went 11–0 and defeated Arkansas 10-3 in the Sugar Bowl to claim the national championship.

Their next three years featured Joe Namath at quarterback and were among Bryant's finest in his career. The 1962 season ended with a 17-0 victory in the Orange Bowl over the University of Oklahoma Sooners. The following year ended with a 12-7 victory over Ole Miss in the 1964 Sugar Bowl, but they lost 21-17 to the University of Texas in the 1965 Orange Bowl, the first nationally televised college game in colour.

Coming off back-to-back national championship seasons, Bryant's Alabama team went undefeated in 1966, and had defeated a strong Nebraska team 34–7 in the Sugar Bowl.

The 1967 team was billed as another national championship contender with star quarterback Kenny Stabler and finished 8–2–1. In 1968, Bryant's team went 8–3, but lost to the University of Missouri 35–10 in the Gator Bowl.

Excited as he was, Brock still had to get through his senior year of high school academics under Coach Bob Harris before finalizing any offer with Coach Bryant and the Crimson Tide.

"Coach Harris didn't smile very much, so he could be kind of scary," remembers Brock of his high school coach. "He was tall, lanky and in great shape. He reminded me of a Marine drill sergeant. You never wanted to get in trouble around Coach Harris."

Friend and former teammate, Pat Patrick also remembers Harris. "Our coaches were hard driving Christians and they expected us to be the same," Patrick said. "We were taught to practice and play hard, respect our opponents, and carry ourselves like we were special."

"Coach Harris told us one day to get a tie and meet him at church the coming Sunday," Patrick said. "Coaches could do that back in those days."

"During the spring game that year, I had hurt my knee," said Brock. "I remember Coach Harris driving by my house numerous times during the summer to see if I was doing my rehab to get ready for my senior season."

"One time when he drove by, I was outside playing basketball," said Brock. "He stopped his car across the street from my house, got out and just stared at me. I could feel it from across the street. He just stood there glaring at me for a few minutes. Then he shook his head and drove off. I went and did my rehab."

As intense and disciplined as his head coach was, Brock still has a great deal of respect for the man. "He was a good coach and I liked him even though Wild Bill had a falling out with him."

But Brock's senior year success did not follow the previous one at Jones Valley and was less than stellar. "Our record during my senior year was bad with only four wins and five losses. We had lost our whole offensive line from the year before and had to replace all five guys," he explained.

"Jimmy Rosser, our All-State and All-American right tackle from the previous year had signed with Alabama and three others had signed with Jacksonville State. We went from having one of the biggest and best offensive lines in the state to having one of the smallest."

"I had recovered well from my knee injury and had a pretty good year throwing the ball," said Brock. "We threw the ball more than anyone else because we were often behind in several games and our running game was not that good. I still had a completion percentage of around 60% and threw twelve touchdowns with only five interceptions the whole year. I also had the longest run ever in my career when I ran an option to the left and ran the ball down the sideline 73 yards for a touchdown."

"I really wanted to go to Alabama and play for Bear Bryant," said Brock. "But I guess after I hurt my knee, things changed and I never heard from them again. That was really disappointing."

But two other schools, Georgia Tech and Auburn had expressed early interest in Brock. "I ended up signing a scholarship what Georgia Tech," he said. "They seemed really interested. I was interested in them because they had signed a former Jones Valley player by the name of Bill Flowers. Bill lived a block away from our house in Green Acres and we grew up together. He was in the same class as Wild Bill so it made sense to me."

Bill Flowers became an All-American linebacker with Georgia Tech and eventually signed with the Dallas Cowboys.

But for Brock, the pieces still weren't falling into place. "I had taken the SAT/ ACT test, but came up a few points shy of getting eligibility into Georgia Tech. I had qualified for other schools, but Georgia Tech really wanted me to take the test again."

Despite the disappointment of his first two choices falling through, Brock had one other option. Auburn was still in the picture. "They came in and offered me their last scholarship, so I accepted their offer."

It was official; Ralph Dieter Brock was on his way to becoming an Auburn quarterback.

In the 1969 Jones Valley Brownie Yearbook, the name Ralph Brock appears on several pages. He received honors and mentions in varsity football, basketball and baseball. He was recognized as All-City Football, All-City Basketball, All-State Football as well as being voted Senior Favourite. And to top it all off, he was the quarterback that led his school to the city championship.

In high school, it doesn't matter how good you are, because it only lasts a short period of time. When it's over, it can either be the start that some young adults embrace or the end that some dread. But while it lasts, if you're good, it can create a kind of glory and adulation that few ever experience and even less fully understand.

Ralph Brock was good, damn good. He was naturally strong, fast, smart and had an arm that could pitch a tight spiral sixty yards downfield without breaking a sweat. The game of football now had an unbreakable hold on him and as his future potential began to unfold, he was not going to let it go.

"I knew that after seeing and playing against other quarterbacks that I was one of the best passers and had one of the best arms around and all I needed was a chance," said Brock.

"Back then, I never had a back-up plan. I never even thought about it. My mind was geared for one thing and one thing only. I had tremendous confidence in my arm," he said.

"I loved the game, but I really knew nothing about what it took to be a good quarterback and I was still scared to death at the thought of failing at it."

Chapter Four

In 1943, George Petrie wrote the Auburn Creed which remains as the cornerstone of the school today.

I believe in education, which gives me the knowledge to work wisely and trains my mind and my hands to work skillfully.

I believe in honesty and truthfulness, without which I cannot win the respect and confidence of my fellow men.

I believe in a sound mind, in a sound body and a spirit that is not afraid, and in clean sports that develop these qualities.

I believe in obedience to law because it protects the rights of all.

I believe in the human touch, which cultivates sympathy with my fellow men and mutual helpfulness and brings happiness for all.

I believe in my Country, because it is a land of freedom and because it is my own home, and that I can best serve that country by "doing justly, loving mercy, and walking humbly with my God."

And because Auburn men and women believe in these things, I believe in Auburn and love it.

Auburn University's history dates back to the pre-Civil War and the Reconstruction era of the South. On February 1, 1856 the Alabama Legislature chartered the East Alabama Male College. Three years later, the school came under the guidance of the Methodist Church and opened its doors to a student body of just eighty and a faculty of ten.

Initially, classes were held in "Old Main" until the college was closed due to the war when most of the students and faculty left to enlist. The campus then became a training ground for the Confederate Army, and "Old Main" served as a hospital for Confederate wounded.

In 1872, the school became the first land-grant college in the South and was renamed the Agricultural and Mechanical College of Alabama. In 1899 the name again was changed, to the Alabama Polytechnic Institute then finally, in 1960, the name of the school was changed to Auburn University.

We all go through transitions in life and certainly the jump from high school to college is unquestionably a big one. Add athletics at a Division 1 school, especially one with a football team like the Auburn Tigers into the mix and that's a lot of change for an 18 year old to handle.

Ralph Brock had graduated from Jones Valley High School in the spring of 1969 with 200 other students. Three months later and 121 miles southeast of Jones Valley High, he was just another one of the 14,525 students attending Auburn.

"I had never been to Auburn before," he said. "I was shocked. My mom and dad drove me down the first day and I checked into Sewell Hall, the football dorm."

"I had signed so late in the year that I never had the chance to see the school or athletic complex," he recalls. "It all just happened so fast."

The Auburn Tigers began competing in intercollegiate football as far back as 1892. Since then, they have collected the 12th most wins in major college history. The NCAA Record Book lists Auburn as National Champions in 1913, 1957, 1983, 1993, and 2010.

The Tigers have won twelve conference championships and twenty-two bowl titles in thirty-nine appearances. They've produced three Heisman Trophy winners: quarterback Pat Sullivan in 1971, running back Bo Jackson in 1985, and quarterback Cam Newton in 2010. Auburn has also produced twenty-nine consensus All-American players. The College Football Hall of Fame has inducted a total of twelve individuals from Auburn, including eight student-athletes and four head coaches: John Heisman, Mike Donahue, Ralph Jordan, and Pat Dye.

Head Coach, Ralph "Shug" Jordan, who coached from 1951 to 1975, led Auburn to a national championship and won a total of 176 games, the most by any Auburn coach.

"I was nervous about all of it," recalls Brock. "The only person I knew was one of my former team mates from Jones Valley, Joe Moon. Auburn had signed him too, but I didn't even know him very well."

The college football environment is far from easy and it's not meant to be. It's not a let's-get-to-know-you gathering, but rather a let's-see-what-you-can-do boot camp. Every player on the team is good, meaning every spot is up for grabs and can be taken at any point.

It doesn't take long for most fresh faced recruits to realize that once they get to college, they've gone from being one of the best high school athletes in their area to hopefully good enough to even get playing time on their college team. They're competing against bigger and faster players, the best of the best. And in the Southeastern Conference, teams like Auburn, Alabama, Tennessee, Louisiana State University, Mississippi, Georgia, Florida, and so on, almost always attract the best high school players in the nation.

From day one, freshmen are immersed into the same program as 21 and 22-year-olds that have already had a few years of experience behind them. In an environment where your worth must be earned, every practice becomes like an All-Star game. It's high powered and intense. The numbers are not on a freshman's side and it's extremely rare for a freshman to be considered one of the best players on the team.

"We had to report the first week of August for fall practice," said Brock. "I was just one of twelve high school quarterbacks that Auburn had signed that year, but several of them were quickly moved to other positions such as defensive back, receivers and so on."

When you step back and think about it from a college coach's point of view, it is a business for them and if you're not performing, you'll be replaced. It's a far cry from high school where a coach could also be your math teacher. In college, coaching is a career, winning is the goal and that makes everything much more intense, disciplined and competitive.

"I used my first practice as a chance to compare myself with all the other quarterbacks, "said Brock. "I knew immediately that I was a much better passer than anybody else and that made me feel a bit more confident. Other than that, we were all just learning the system and techniques that the coaches wanted."

"Almost all the athletes lived in Sewell Hall and our schedules were set," said Brock. "Breakfast would be served between 6:30 and 7:45. My first class was at 8:00am, so I'd get up around 7:00am. I had two more classes before lunch which was served between 11:30 and 12:45. After lunch, I had maybe 45 minutes to relax before heading over to a 1:45 quarterback meeting to watch film and go over the playbook. After that, we would get dressed for a two hour practice. Between practice, game film and studying, there wasn't much free time."

Even in the early days of that first camp, Brock was being noticed. "Coach Hilyer had said that I was the best quarterback they had signed," recalled Brock. "I fit in well with all the freshmen that had come in that season, but when it came to having to scrimmage against the varsity football team, that was another story. I realized the hard way how fast these varsity players were. I had never been hit so hard as I had that first day on the field."

"In those days, freshmen could not play on the varsity team," said Brock. "So I was assigned to the freshman team with the other quarterbacks, but after they moved several of them to other positions, it left four of us to actually play quarterback."

"The first game I played in was against Florida. I threw five passes and completed four with three touchdowns of 50 yards or better with limited playing time. The next game was against the University of Georgia. Our only touchdown was when I threw a touchdown pass, but again, I saw limited action and we lost that game 19-6. It was our only loss of the freshman season. But rumours were getting out how good I was throwing the ball and how strong my arm was."

"After the first two games, I was the leading passer on the freshman team, but I had probably only played a total of one half of football. "

"Our third game was against the Mississippi State Bulldogs in Starkville, Mississippi," he continued. Brock's two limited performances before the Mississippi game were notable and his confidence was building with every pass and every yard gained. "I had thrown four touchdown passes with no interceptions in the last two games, so of course I was expecting to play quite a bit in Starkville."

"Well, it's halftime and I still hadn't gotten on the field," said Brock, frustrated with the situation. "We were leading 7-0 going into the third quarter. We kicked a field goal which extended our lead to 10, but it's getting late in the third quarter. Another player, Terry Henley, a running back, hadn't been put in either. "

"Terry and I were talking to each other on the bench and saying if we don't get in by the start of the fourth quarter, we were not going in at all, even if they told us to," said Brock. "By the way, Henley became a really good running back at Auburn, being named first team All SEC in 1972 and signing a pro contract with the Atlanta Falcons in 1973 after he graduated."

"Well, it's into the fourth quarter and we're still not in the game," said Brock. "So we both go to the far end of the bench and sit there telling each other we're not going in. Then, here comes the freshman coach telling me it's time for me to go in. But I know at this time that all I will be doing is running the clock out so I told him no, I wasn't going in. He walked away and about a minute or so later came back and told Henley to go in. Henley jumped up and went into the ball game after we had agreed not to."

"After the game I quietly got dressed and got on the bus. I was really mad because again, I wasn't given an opportunity to play in a meaningful situation," Brock said. "On the bus ride home, the coach came and sat down beside me and told me that I am going to play the whole game the following week."

With a 2-1 record, the freshman Tigers were set to play the University of Mississippi's Ole Miss Rebels and Ralph Brock was assigned the starting quarterback position. "Just like the coach said, I played the whole game against Mississippi. He was letting me throw the football, but we are behind 6-0 going into the fourth quarter. I had already thrown for over 200 yards, but we just couldn't score any points."

"I had wanted an opportunity to play in a meaningful situation and now this was it. They handed it to me. I pulled myself away for a moment and told myself that I had to do something."

No one knows if it's a mystery or a science, but there are moments when an athlete's instinct takes over and everything just clicks. "On third down from our own 25-yard line, I dropped back and threw a deep ball. Our receiver caught the 75-yard touchdown pass. We kicked the extra point and won the game 7-6," said Brock. "In the end, I completed 20 of 35 passes for almost 300 yards in the game."

The Auburn Tigers finished the 1969 season with a 4-1 record.

"I think I realized after my first year at Auburn and especially going into my sophomore year that I had the physical ability to play professional football," said Brock. "I had watched and studied the varsity quarterback, Pat Sullivan throwing the football. I studied all the other quarterbacks at Auburn and around the Southeastern Conference. I knew that I could throw the football better than those guys, but I just needed a chance."

Just like Brock, varsity quarterback, Pat Sullivan had also come from Birmingham and was a three-sport high school star. Sullivan had also chosen to play football for Auburn University, and in 1969, he became the starting quarterback under Head Coach Ralph Jordan. Over the next three seasons, he broke school and NCAA records for passing while leading the team to a 26–7 record.

In 1970, Sullivan led the NCAA in total offence with 2,856 yards and set an NCAA record for most yards per play with 8.57. In his college career, he was responsible for

71 touchdowns; 53 passing and 18 rushing touchdowns to tie the NCAA record. In his senior season, Sullivan completed 162 passes on 281 attempts for 2,012 yards and 20 touchdowns and won the 1971 Heisman Trophy.

After college, in 1972, Sullivan was a 2nd round selection in the NFL Draft chosen by the Atlanta Falcons. He played with the Falcons from 1972 to 1976 and then the Washington Redskins in 1976 and 1977.

"I felt I was better than Sullivan, but I hadn't had the opportunity to prove that yet," said Brock. "The next season I was a red shirt sophomore. That means I got an extra year to play because they are holding me out to give me two years of playing after Pat Sullivan had graduated."

Larry Willingham was an All-American defensive back at Auburn in 1970 and remembers Brock as a freshman. "Ralph ran the scout team offence against us in practice," said Willingham. "I remember one practice I was covering one of the receivers about 40 yards downfield and was hit by one of his passes. It hit me in the bicep and my whole arm went numb and dropped. Coach yelled at me from the sideline something about why I didn't catch it and I yelled back, 'You come out here and try to handle one of those!'"

After college, Willingham was drafted in the fourth round by the St. Louis Cardinals that year. He played two years with them before moving on to the World Football League for both the Birmingham Americans in 1974 and the Birmingham Vulcans in 1975. He was inducted into the Alabama Sports Hall of Fame in 2003.

Ralph Brock's arm strength was being noticed by coaches as well. "Word was getting out that I had the best arm ever at Auburn. The varsity quarterback coach was a man name Bobby Freeman. I think Winnipeg wanted to sign him back in the 50s or 60s to be their quarterback, but he ended up signing with the Philadelphia Eagles instead. Coach Freeman told me I had a better arm than Sonny Jurgensen, the NFL Hall of Fame quarterback that he had played with," said Brock. "And our defensive backfield coach Bill Oliver said I had a better arm then Bert Jones who was playing at LSU. I really just needed the opportunity to play and show everybody that I could be successful at not just throwing the football, but playing the game."

"One day we were doing a seven-on-seven passing drill where the scout team would service the defence for the upcoming varsity game against LSU," said Brock. "I'm quarterbacking the scout team and Coach Oliver yells out to the defence that we are going against the best arm in the Southeastern Conference. And he was pointing at me. I thought that was quite the compliment because I thought Bert Jones, the quarterback at LSU who was drafted number one by the Baltimore Colts had, in my opinion, the best arm I had seen."

"I remember during one practice, one of the receivers ran a 12 yard hook pattern and I let the ball go. I was trying to time it up for him, but as soon as he turned around, the ball struck him in his face mask. They had to stop practice and to pry the ball out of his helmet. I was hitting receivers 80 to 85 yards downfield in stride and everyone was noticing."

"But football was the easy part for me," remembers Brock. "It was being homesick that was tough. I missed all my buddies from around the neighbourhood. I didn't know very many people, if any at Auburn, so I was quite lonely."

Growing up, Brock was never one to make friends easily. He was quiet and shy, often mistaken as aloof or even stuck up. He had his tight group of friends from the neighbourhood and that was enough for him. "As long as I was playing football I was fine, but as soon as I left the playing field, I was ready to go home. I didn't have any friends at Auburn. My roommate and weren't close at all. All I wanted to do was play football and study."

"Financially, I didn't have to spend very much money on anything. My mom and dad would send me some spending money every week and Auburn had a laundry money allowance so I was good there. But when it came to having any free time at all, I was ready to head back to Birmingham and my friends. I didn't have a car that first year so after the football season was over I would leave school on Fridays and hitchhike all the way back to Birmingham 120 miles. Sometimes it would take me eight to ten different rides to get back home."

While some students delight in college life away from the classroom and the books, Brock was an exception to that rule. Late night parties and drinking didn't interest him in least. "I didn't drink alcohol at all back then which I learned can be a big part of college life. I saw my dad drink when I was growing up and at times he got pretty mean. Deep down, I was afraid that if I started drinking, it might affect me the same way and that scared me."

"When I first got to Auburn, all the other players were drinking and partying, but I didn't. I really had nothing in common with them except football and that's all I was interested in. After the football season was over, I just didn't fit in."

"During my freshman year, one night my next door roommates were tanked up drinking whiskey and beer. They came banging on my door around 2:00am. It was Terry Beasley, an All-American wide receiver who was the first round draft choice of the San Francisco 49ers and his roommate, Frank Dixon. On the field, Beasley was the fastest receiver I had ever seen. He wasn't very big, maybe 5' 11," and 185lb but he was strong as hell," he recalled.

"They scared the hell out of me. I didn't know what to think. They were saying 'Here have a drink! Here have a drink!' So I did. That was when I first began to drink and I realized I liked beer."

For better or worse, the place where one grows up usually will always retain an iconic status in one's heart and mind. It's human nature to want to have a place to belong, but it also has to be a place that defines the person.

"There were three or four times that when I did go home, I wasn't sure I was going to go back to Auburn," said Brock. "One time I had to get my parents to take me back. Another time my uncle, who was a retired Marine with his flying license, flew me back in a small plane. I was picked up by Coach Hilyer at the airport in Auburn."

"It made things a little easier once I got a car. It was a little 1967 Blue Volkswagen Beetle and I was able to get around more, but I still wasn't comfortable off the field. I always wanted to just go home. "

In the words of poet Robert Frost, "Home is the place that, when you have to go there, they have to take you in." For most, good or bad, home can be the center of one's world and a place of order that contrasts the chaos and insecurity elsewhere. Home is that place where one feels in control; it is a predictable and secure place. It is the primary connection between an individual and the rest of the world.

"On one trip home, I ran into one of my high school friends, Johnny Colburn," said Brock. "Instead of college, Johnny ended up going to Vietnam after high school and he was back in Birmingham. His nickname was "Houzer" because we used to take things and say they were on the house. Of course they weren't."

"Johnny, Wild Bill, Fats and I decided to take a trip to Panama City, Florida for a week. We packed fifteen cases of beer into the Beetle along with the four of us. The car was packed and we could barely move. We would have to gain speed going down hills just to get the momentum we needed to get up the other side on the interstate."

"I think we had $90 between all the four us and the hotel room was $48 for four days. The rest of the money was used for beer, beer and more beer. I think it was $0.99 for a six pack of beer, so we drank a lot of beer."

"Between beer, gas and the hotel room, there wasn't any money left for food. Our plan for eating was to hit one of the restaurants on the strip. We would park our car four or five blocks away and walk down to the restaurant. Everybody was ordering whatever they wanted, but not overeating so that you would have the ability to run as fast as we could for our escape. One or two of us would act like we were going to the restroom, while the others would act like they're waiting for the bill. When the waitress got out of sight, we bolted out the back door and down the beach to our car."

"When I was home we did other crazy things like sneaking into movie theaters and sporting events, but a lot of times we would just get a six-pack of beer and drive around listening to music and shooting the shit."

Back at Auburn, with football back in the forefront, Brock's standing with the program was starting to rise. After leading the freshman team to a successful 4-1 season in the previous year, it was time to move up a level.

"I was assigned to backup Sullivan on the varsity team in 1971. I knew I was a better passer than Sullivan, but I also knew that he was an established quarterback and no matter how good I was or anyone else was, he was going to be the quarterback and I understood that. I just wanted the opportunity to throw the ball a little bit if or when I got in the game."

On October 23, 1971, in front of 55,000 spectators at Cliff Hare Stadium in Auburn, Ralph Brock would get his opportunity. "We were playing Clemson and leading 35-6. We've had the game won already when they put me in so it really didn't matter. They just wanted me to run the clock down, but I had a different idea. I wanted to throw the football. That's what I do. It's who I am."

And with little time left on the play clock, that's exactly what Brock did. "I called pass in the huddle and threw a 40-yard bullet down the left sideline, but it landed right in the chest of the Clemson defensive back. He couldn't help but catch it. I gave it to him and he returned the ball for a touchdown."

"I don't know, maybe I'm just wired differently," said Brock solemnly. "If I had been told to run a running play, I would have run a running play. But I wasn't told what play to run. I guess it was expected of me, as a quarterback, when you have a lead and the clock's running down, you should just run the clock out. But good players, when they get into the game, want to play. At least I did."

The reaction of his head coach still haunts Brock. "As I came off the field, Coach Jordan started yelling at the offensive coordinator to get me the hell out of the game."

One would assume the embarrassment of being called out in front of 55,000 people in the stands and in front of his teammates would be enough, but his punishment still wasn't over.

"The next day at the quarterback meeting, Coach Freeman told me in front of the other quarterbacks that I was being dropped back down to the third team and that the third team quarterback Ted Smith, would now backup Sullivan."

"I'm not saying he was wrong for dropping me, but if it was me, I would have pulled the player aside and explained the situation to him and why they were doing this."

"After that meeting, while everyone was getting dressed and ready for that day's practice, I packed up my stuff and loaded the Beetle. I was leaving Auburn. I stopped by the Practice Facility for a moment, and watched them just long enough to wave goodbye."

Chapter Five

It can be a long lonely road of doubt and uncertainty when one doesn't know the next step forward. As the young quarterback drove away from Auburn University, making his way down U.S Highway 280-E back towards Birmingham, he desperately tried to come up with a plan.

"I didn't know what I was going to do," Brock said, remembering the drive from Auburn. "I didn't have a plan B. I had no idea where I was going to go. But there was one thing I was certain of, I wasn't going home. I couldn't. I knew my dad would be furious and demand that I get my ass back to Auburn."

"I drove to Jacksonville State which is about two hours north of Auburn. I had a few high school teammates still playing there. I thought maybe I could find some answers there. If nothing else, maybe some support."

Jacksonville State University is located in Jacksonville, Alabama, 110 miles north of Auburn and 75 miles southwest east of Birmingham. The university was founded in 1883 as Jacksonville State Normal School. In 1930 the name changed to Jacksonville State Teachers College, and then again in 1957 to Jacksonville State College.

The school had participated in the original Mid-South Conference with six other universities in the summer of 1970: Delta State, Florence State (now North Alabama), Jacksonville State, Livingston (now West Alabama), Tennessee–Martin, and Troy State (now Troy).

In 1971, the league changed its name to the Gulf South Conference and added Southeastern Louisiana and Nicholls State, increasing the membership to eight schools.

"When I first got to Jacksonville, I couldn't find anybody," said Brock. "It was like the whole school had closed down."

He knew he had to buy time, time to think and figure out what his next step would be.

"I was still afraid to go home, but I drove back to Birmingham anyway. I checked into a cheap motel," said Brock. At that time, the Birmingham Inn was $10 a night and was exactly what one would expect for that kind of money. "It wasn't very nice, but it was close to my house."

He settled in, assuming he could work through his options before making any decisions, but unfortunately his secret wouldn't be safe for long.

"The next morning, I picked up the Birmingham newspaper and saw it."

The exact headline in the Anniston Star was;

"Brock quits Auburn team."

In the Associated Press article, Coach Shug Jordan, Auburn's head coach was quoted as saying, "Brock had left for reasons all his own. We're sorry he's given up football."

But Brock hadn't given up football despite what was printed in the news. All he wanted was a chance to play and he just didn't feel that was going to happen at Auburn.

"I panicked," said Brock. "Not about playing football, but about going home. Now I had no choice. I knew my dad would see it. Eventually I made my way home and sure enough, he was mad as hell. He gave me two options; go back to Auburn or enlist in the Army."

"But before I could really do anything, Pat Sullivan was on the phone. He called me and asked me to come back. And then Coach Jordan called. They all wanted me to come back." Why? Because Sullivan was in his last year and Ralph Brock had being set as Auburn's future starting quarterback.

"The next day my dad and I drove back to Auburn to see Coach Jordan," said Brock. "I honestly don't remember ever having much of a conversation with Coach during the two and a half years I was at Auburn. This was actually the first time that I was going to be sitting down with the head coach to talk."

"The reason why I was allowed to come back and talk to him was because the offensive coaches, especially Coach Freeman and the receiver coach really liked me," said Brock. "They thought I could develop into a good quarterback. I assumed they were going to run the same kind of offence that Pat Sullivan had been running and I would have been a good fit."

"I don't remember exactly what was said except that Coach Jordan informed us he wanted me back, but I had lost my scholarship for leaving and we would have to pay for the next two quarters of school."

"I don't recall any promises about any playing time or anything else, but I knew right away when he said we would have to pay, that was it. We didn't have that kind of money, so I was done with Auburn."

But if Auburn wasn't going to work out, Brock knew there had to be other schools that would take him. "I thought about Troy State because they had a good passing game and they had tried real hard to get me when I was a freshman at Auburn. They knew I was unhappy there."

"One of my high school receivers from Jones Valley, Hassel Walls, was a receiver at Jacksonville State. He was the older brother of "Fats." He introduced me to Coach Charley Pell and Clarkie Mayfield, the offensive coordinator when they were playing a game in Birmingham a couple of weeks later. The quarterback at Jacksonville State was Doc Lett and he had been a four-year starter. He was graduating after that year so they were looking for another quarterback.

"They had already signed a quarterback, Buddy Talley, who had transferred from the University of Alabama. He was supposed to have been a really outstanding passer," said Brock. "But Coach Pell offered me a full scholarship which meant I would have two years to play at Jax State."

"I felt comfortable at Jacksonville State right from the beginning. The coaches were great and I knew some of the players. On top of that, Wild Bill was going to school there," said Brock, happy to be back among friends.

"Plus Birmingham was only a little over an hour away. This was the first time in three years I really felt comfortable."

Something else would happen to Brock in his early days at the new school. Insignificant to some, the opportunity meant a lot to the young quarterback. "I never had the chance to choose my number in high school or when I went to Auburn. It was always assigned to me. I had always wanted number 5 because that was Joe DiMaggio's number. Joe was a great baseball player and a hero of mine going up. Wearing number 5 was also different from what the other quarterbacks were wearing at the time. They gave me number 5 and I've worn it ever since."

Once it was confirmed that Brock was to become a Jacksonville State Gamecock, Auburn's head coach was quoted in the press saying he knew that Brock had an arm the day he overthrew Terry Beasley by 20 yards. He also said Brock should burn the Gulf South league up. Tom Jones, who had also coached Brock as a freshman at Auburn was quoted in the same article, saying, "Ralph Brock has one of the finest arms I've ever seen."

But despite the hype, his first spring appearance with the Jacksonville State Gamecocks was not impressive. Brock threw 24 passes for just 115 yards. But immediately after the game, Coach Pell still believed in him and announced Ralph Brock would be the Gamecock's No 1 starter going into the fall season. Coach Pell had seen something he liked.

"I end up being the starting quarterback at Jacksonville State in 1972," said Brock. "I just wanted the opportunity to play and show them I was a good overall quarterback and not just a great arm."

In his first appearance of the fall season, Brock led the team to 490 yards of offence and a victory against Nicholls State.

By mid-September, he was the leading passer in the league and under his leadership; the Gamecocks led the entire league in passing offence. As a team, they placed second in rushing and total offence. In a short period of time, Brock had made an impression and was now being described as having the ability to be the best small college passer in the country.

Rudy Abbott, who wrote for the local Jacksonville newspaper wrote a description of Brock that still remains today. "Ralph Brock can throw a football through a car wash without getting it wet."

After three weeks, he continued setting the pace for the entire league averaging 179.3 yards per game and a passing offence average of 13 passes per game.

On November 21, 1972, Ralph Brock was named player of the week in the Gulf South Conference for his outstanding performance against Florence State. He had completed 15 of 26 passes with four touchdowns in a 39-20 come from behind victory.

With a record of 7-3, Head Coach Pell was questioned by the local media about the success of the season and his quarterback. "Why such a gifted athlete would choose to play small college football was the reason people were talking about Ralph Brock."

Going into the 1973 season, a poll of the Gulf South coaches had the Jaxmen finishing in fourth place. Coach Pell was not disappointed with the low ranking his team had received because he knew what they had. He wasn't quite ready to put a championship label on the season yet, but he was extremely happy with his quarterback position.

"We have an unusual and promising situation at quarterback for the first time in the five years I've been here," Pell told the Anniston Star on August 5, 1973. "We have exceptional depth and talent. He's (Brock) an all-star candidate with professional ability and exceptional talent."

Assistant coach and offensive coordinator, Clarkie Mayfield also told the press "He's all quarterback. He has the finest arm on any quarterback I've ever seen and that includes people I've played with or against such as Rick Norton, George Mira, Fran Tarkenton and a bunch of others."

Going into the 1973 season, Brock hadn't missed a step from the previous season. By September he was third in offence in the league and second in passing with 126 yards. He was once again named offensive player of the week after tying his own conference passing record against Nicholls State with four touchdowns after a 28-10 win.

A month later, Brock led the Gulf South Conference in passing and was considered one of the top ten quarterback prospects in the country with 30 completions on 39 attempts, 418 yards and seven touchdowns. Coach Pell was quoted as saying he wouldn't "trade Brock for any quarterback in the country. Don't you know Auburn would like to have him back now."

On October 13, Brock broke the Conference's game record by hitting 13 completions on 18 attempts for 161 yards against SLU.

The entire Jacksonville State University's 1973 football team had put a dent in the Gamecocks' record book. They went 7-2-0 and ended the season as the number four team in the country. Ralph Brock averaged 35.4 points per game beating the old record of 32.5 set by the JSU's 1970 undefeated team. JSU's point total of 319 also set a new high and ranked Jacksonville third in the country in scoring for all small colleges.

Personally, Brock had hit for 17 touchdowns and ran for five more, setting more new records for the school. His four touchdown performances against Nicholls State and Northeast Louisiana tied his old mark set in the year before. He also established a new high with ten straight completions in one game.

In his two years with Jacksonville State, Ralph Brock had led his team to an impressive 14-4 record, but his next performance was one that he had never anticipated.

He was a surprised when Assistant Coach Mayfield called and informed him of the news. "Son, you're in the Senior Bowl." Ralph Brock would be the first Jacksonville State footballer to ever be invited to play in the Mobile, Alabama Pro Classic game for college players.

"That was a shock," said Brock. "The Senior Bowl is where the top college players in the nation are invited and now I was one of them. I had no regrets about leaving Auburn. I just wanted the opportunity to play football and I got that at Jacksonville."

For college football, the season comes to an end in Mobile, Alabama at the Senior Bowl. But for professional football, the season reaches a climax in Mobile in what was better known as Super Sunday. The best of the 1973 college players would clash on January 12, 1974 in front of professional coaches, scouts and general managers.

"That was the biggest honour I'd ever received," said Brock. "I was really excited about going and knew it was probably the best opportunity I'd ever have."

Brock had received questionnaires from six different National Football League teams interested in his services. He'd also had contact with a few teams from the Canadian Football League and the upstart World Football League.

Two quarterbacks had been chosen to represent the South squad in that year's Senior Bowl; Ralph Brock and Arizona State's Danny White. White had already appeared in two post season all-star games that season; first in the East-West Shrine game held in San Francisco, and the second in the Hula Bowl in Hawaii the week before the Senior Bowl.

Brock had not played since Jacksonville State's win against Florence State in mid-November and because of that, White was chosen as the squad's starter.

Don McCafferty, the head coach for the Detroit Lions was the head coach for the south squad. He was quoted as saying, "Boy, that Brock can hum a football. There's no doubt in my mind that he can throw. But his height would be a major concern. And coming from a small school, a lot of people wouldn't have heard of him. But he deserves his recognition."

"When I first arrived, especially after our first practice, I looked up at all those big guys and asked myself what was I was doing here," said Brock. "I wanted to do well, but not just for myself, for Jax State and the coaching staff. I wanted to make them proud. I figured if I could do well, maybe someone else from the school would get the chance to play in future Senior Bowl games."

With White playing the entire first half of the game, the South was slow at putting points on the board. But when Brock went in, he did his thing right off the bat. His first pass attempt missed the receiver who couldn't get to the ball in time, but on his third play, he scrambled for seven yards and a first down.

With 12:10 remaining in the fourth quarter, Brock made a perfect pitch for a touchdown. The capacity crowd of 40,646 saw the South take its first lead of the game, 13-9.

But USC's Lynn Swann would take over on the game's final drive as the North went 80 yards on eight plays. Heisman Trophy winner John Cappelletti of Penn State, who gained 201 yards rushing and receiving on the day, gave the North a first down on the South 17 with a 16-yard reception. Then with less than 30 seconds to go in the game, Lynn Swann made his game-winning catch giving the North squad the 16-13 win.

"To be honest, I didn't think I had a very good Senior Bowl. I was disappointed in myself," said Brock. "I hadn't really worked out since the Florence game. I had a good arm, but I didn't know very much about what it took to be a professional quarterback. I relied on talent alone throwing the football, but there's way more to being a good quarterback than just throwing the ball. I didn't know much about reading defences and I really didn't figure that out until later."

"But after my year at Jacksonville State and the Senior Bowl, I had confidence in my arm," said Brock. "I was tough and naturally strong, but I was not very big at a little over 6' and 190 pounds."

"I just wanted the opportunity," said Brock. "I definitely wanted to play pro football, regardless of which team or league. I had no preference on where I wanted to play, I just wanted to play. "

"It was Bud Riley who first approached me about coming to Winnipeg," said Brock. "It was at the Senior Bowl he told me a bit about the Canadian Football League."

Edward Jones "Bud" Riley, Jr, had just been appointed the head coach for the CFL's Winnipeg Blue Bombers. Riley was born and raised in Guin, Alabama so there was an immediate connection between the two.

"I didn't know much about the league or Canada," said Brock. "I had watched a couple games on TV at Jacksonville, but that was about it."

"But I wanted to wait until after the NFL draft," said Brock. "Bud came to Birmingham and took me out to dinner. I told him I was going to wait, but then the World Football League held their draft a week later. They drafted like ten quarterbacks in the first few rounds and I wasn't one of them. My name wasn't even mentioned."

"Two weeks later, Bud made the second offer by phone. I was surprised because it was better than the first. I told him to let me think about it."

Most would have missed it if they weren't paying attention. On Tuesday January 29, 1974, below the Associated Press' headline announcing Muhammad Ali's defeat of Joe Frazier in the Anniston Star, under a small headline in the bottom right hand column, the article read;

Canadian Club gets Jax' Brock

Quarterback Ralph Brock of Jacksonville State has signed a professional contract with Winnipeg of the Canadian Football League.

"I feel good about it," Brock said. "I don't think I could have found a better deal anywhere," said Brock. Details of the deal were not disclosed.

Brock passed for 1293 yards and 17 touchdowns for Jacksonville and led the south to its only touchdown in the senior bowl game at Mobile.

Everyone who knows Ralph knows he's a winner and we wish him the best of luck in Winnipeg," said Coach Charley Pell of Jacksonville.

"I think it's somewhere just north of North Dakota," Brock said. "I know it's about 80 miles from the border."

Why? "Well I just didn't see how I could get any better offer from the NFL or the WFL so I decided not to wait."

"I knew from everything that was being said about me as a passer and from everything I had seen from playing against other quarterbacks, I had one of the best arms in football and all I needed was a chance."

"I was a physical education major, but was a few hours short of getting my degree at Jacksonville State. I left school with one thing in mind and that was to play professional football."

"When Bud came back and upped his original offer, that's really when I decided not to wait for the NFL draft. I didn't want to lose my chance. My mind was now geared for one thing, making it in Winnipeg."

Chapter Six

Back in mid-November 1973, around the same time Ralph Brock was packing up his football gear from his Jacksonville State locker for the last time, a similar exercise was taking place 2,400 kilometers north in Winnipeg, Canada.

Jim Spavital, the Winnipeg Blue Bombers' head coach, was packing up his effects at the club's Maroons Road office. Spavital had coached his last season with the Canadian Football League's team, compiling a record of 23-39-2, with just two playoff appearances in four years.

When he first appeared in Winnipeg in 1970, Spavital took over the reins of a mediocre football team whose glory days were quickly fading into the past. Professional sports can be an unforgiving journey and the 58 year old coach had become just another milestone in the team's history.

The Winnipeg Blue Bombers' glory days had started in the early 1950s and were led by legendary head coach, Bud Grant. During Grant's tenure, the Blue Bombers featured the likes of Ken Ploen, Leo Lewis, Ernie Pitts, and Ed Kotowich on the roster. The Blue Bombers competed in six Grey Cup games during Grant's term, winning four of them in 1958, 1959, 1961, and 1962.

During the second half of the 1960s, the Blue Bombers' supremacy in the CFL was fading, with four seasons of double digits in the loss column. The team seemed to bounce back in the early 1970s under Jim Spavital with the likes of quarterback Don Jonas, running-back Mack Herron, and wide receivers Jim Thorpe, and Bob LaRose. In 1972 Spavital led the team to a first place finish in the

Western Conference, but the team came up short in the Western Final against the Saskatchewan Roughriders.

The following year, the Blue Bombers posted a dismal record of 4-11-1 and Head Coach Jim Spavital, with a year still remaining on his contract, was sent packing.

Blue Bombers' general manager, Earl Lunsford and the team's management group had cited several areas of concern against the head coach. They claimed game preparation, a deteriorating rapport with players and a weak selection of personnel were three key faults against Spavital.

On December 9, 1973, Lunsford introduced Bud Riley as the new Blue Bombers' head coach. Riley, an Alabamian, had been an assistant with the Saskatchewan Roughriders for the 1973 season after eight highly productive seasons as the defensive coordinator at Oregon State. He had ten years of coaching high school football in Idaho and Lunsford and Riley had known each other since the mid-60s.

With a two year contract in place, Riley was expected to make the Winnipeg Blue Bombers a force in the league and he didn't consider it an impossible task. "We have some fine football players here," he was quoted as saying. "This team just didn't make the big play at the right time, but there's a good nucleus here."

When asked about the team's quarterback situation, Riley had said, "I think Don Jonas is a fine quarterback and he can continue to be. He had problems with shifting personnel, but he showed us consistency later on."

"I'm not worrying about hurting Don's feelings, but I also have no intention of taking the game away from my quarterback."

But thirty-two days later, Coach Riley introduced himself to a new young quarterback at the Mobile, Alabama Senior Bowl.

When you consider the timing of it all, it's hard to fathom just how fast Riley had moved in on the young prospect. Few people knew that Riley had actually been tipped off about Brock by the staff from Jacksonville State during a coach's convention in San Francisco. On a scouting trip at Clemson a few weeks later, he dropped by Jacksonville State and watched game film on the young quarterback.

His next move was to head down to the Senior Bowl to see how Ralph Brock performed on the field in an actual game situation. But, even though Brock hadn't played much in the game, Riley was impressed with what he had seen and heard.

"I remember Coach Riley telling me about Don Jonas and the CFL," said Brock. "I think he said something like the guy had played sixteen years and the team didn't really have a back-up. One of the players that stepped in as a back-up was actually a receiver."

"When I didn't get drafted in the World Football League, the first Winnipeg offer was looking pretty good," Brock said. "But when the offer went up the second time, I felt like that was what I needed to do."

"I didn't have an agent or advisor, so I was kind of unsure about everything at the time. I didn't get any direction or advice from the coaches at Jacksonville State. I was really on my own about the whole process. I did talk to my dad and got his advice, somewhat, but I took the chance and signed with Winnipeg before the NFL draft," he recalled.

"In retrospect, I probably should have waited until after the NFL draft, which was about a month or two away, but I didn't want to lose the offer from Winnipeg. I wanted to play football so I signed the contract offer from the Blue Bombers for one year at $24,000 plus a signing bonus of $7,500." The average CFL salary in 1973 was $26,000, surprisingly just $1,000 less than the National Football League average. "I was happy with what I got."

But certain people in the NFL weren't happy with his decision. Coming from a small school, Brock's evaluation by the NFL scouts and coaches was not high on their lists. From what little they had seen and heard, they were impressed with his leadership and arm strength and had wanted to see more. But once he had agreed to the Winnipeg contract, Brock was forgotten.

He arrived in Winnipeg on May 16, 1974, just six days after he and his new wife, Kathy, had exchanged wedding vows in Birmingham.

"I remember driving up to Winnipeg that first time and thinking how flat it was," he recalled. "We found an apartment across from the University of Manitoba."

"I came up early that first year. I'm sure everybody thought I was crazy," he said. "But there was a lot to learn. I had to learn their system and learn about the other quarterbacks and players on the team. I knew nothing about the league or about defences. I still hadn't figured out what it took to become a professional quarterback. I just committed to making the team and the one thing that I had going for me was my throwing ability."

Bud Riley had been in the coaching business long enough to know that first impressions really didn't mean much, but he was convinced that Brock had one of the finest throwing arms he had seen. He saw the potential in the young quarterback and showing up more than a month before everyone else was a good indication that Brock was hungry for a spot on his roster.

The official start of the Blue Bombers' training was still a week away when the team's other prospective quarterbacks reported to Winnipeg Stadium. The group included 1973 back-up, Tommy Pharr and newcomers Steve Endicott, D.C. Nobles, Kelly Cochrane and Ralph Brock.

Steve Endicott had played for Riley at Oregon State and had a promising career ahead of him until he broke a bone in his throwing hand as a junior. He hadn't been able to perform as a senior, so the professional scouts forgot about him.

Endicott had approached Riley prior to the camp and asked for a shot with Blue Bombers. That's all Riley needed to hear. In the early days of camp, Endicott had been throwing the ball with force and precision.

The University of Houston's standout star, D.C. Nobles, was also in attendance. Months before, Nobles had been hailed as the team's top off season acquisition. Most of the media attention was set on Nobles, who had received a substantial signing bonus, but it was evident early on that he hadn't been physically prepared before arriving.

"D. C. Nobles was the guy I believe the Bombers thought was going to be their backup to Don Jonas," said Brock. "I remember he showed up to camp in a nice shiny Lincoln Continental with the license plate, "DC QB.""

"There was another quarterback from Mississippi State, Tommy Pharr. He was the backup to Don Jonas, I think from 1972 until I got there. "Kelly Cochrane was from Miami and he had the ability to play defence as well."

The quarterbacks spent five hours a day going over the Blue Bomber playbook with offensive coach, Fred Hightower, before being turned loose on the field with bags of footballs. Their schedule would continue for the following seven days until the official start of training camp. It wasn't a produce or else situation, because none of them were expected to be in the first round of cuts.

On day one, Brock began establishing himself and continued to make an impression when camp shifted to St. Johns Ravenscourt School, the team's training camp headquarters.

"It helped having one of my former teammates, Terry Owens from Jacksonville State there for at least the first week or two of training camp. And, of course, there were some other players that Riley had brought up from Alabama. My whole thought process was just to make the team as the backup quarterback."

On June 16, 1974, the Winnipeg Blue Bombers' training camp was officially underway. But this camp would be different from previous years. The first and only CFL players' strike in league history was in full swing. The Players Association was holding out, meaning most veterans were not reporting to their respective training camps. 270 of the league's 288 veteran players had filed retirement papers and stayed away, leaving only rookies as participants.

The CFL Players Association was seeking a minimum salary of $11,000 a year for players. They also wanted each veteran to receive $17 a day for the 44 days of training camp compared to the $10 from the previous years.

For preseason games, the Players Association wanted $150 per game for each veteran compared to the $50 they had been used to receiving.

The association also wanted each player on the 1974 Grey Cup winning team to receive a $6,000 bonus compared to $3,000 and for the losing team; each player was to receive $3,000 compared to the previous $2,000.

The CFL strike coincided with a similarly timed strike in the National Football League, which became one of the key factors in the success of establishing the existence of the World Football League in the U.S.

Three weeks of training camp had passed before the league and players' association eventually agreed to a three-year deal including a minimum salary of $11,000, increased pre- and post-season compensation, increased pension contributions and medical protection.

Just a few days into the Blue Bombers' official training camp, Brock had set himself number one in the quarterback position followed by Endicott, Cochrane and Nobles. The highly touted Nobles had excelled at play action passes and roll outs, but didn't have a very strong arm for drop backs which lowered his value to the team. It was obvious that Endicott's hand still had not completed healed from his previous injury.

By late June, Cochrane and Endicott were placed on waivers and eventually Cochrane was dealt to Montreal.

The entire atmosphere changed when the veterans finally reported to camp after the players' strike had ended. "When I saw Bill Frank for the first time, he scared me," said Brock. "He was so big, intimidating and tough-looking. I kept thinking, how could I ever to be comfortable in the same huddle with this guy?"

"In the beginning, huddles were difficult for him," recalled John Bonk, the CFL Hall of Fame center. "You could tell his confidence wasn't there, yet. And most of the time, we couldn't understand what he was saying because of his accent."

Of all the veterans who reported to camp, one of the biggest names was quarterback, Don Jonas. The veteran quarterback had been named the CFL's Most Outstanding

Player in 1971 and was a league all-star in both '71 and '72. The Penn State graduate had completed 253 of 485 passes for 4,036 yards in his award winning season. He also threw 27 touchdown passes. Jonas had thrown for more than 3,000 yards a year for three straight seasons with the Blue Bombers.

"I remember seeing him for the first time and thinking what good shape he was in. Being a rookie, I didn't get to know him very well, but he had great confidence on the field."

All through training camp, Brock worked at establishing himself as Jonas' back-up and it was no surprise when Riley announced that he would be the starting in the team's first preseason game against the Montreal Alouettes.

Despite a 23-8 loss, Brock showed poise and threw the ball well, completing nine passes on eighteen attempts for one-hundred-eleven yards. According to reports, he was calm, cool and collected in his professional debut.

Nobles on the other hand, didn't fare quite as well completing just one pass on his four attempts, finishing his time on the field with a negative three yards of offence and one interception.

With only a few days of training camp under his belt, Don Jonas saw limited action against the Alouettes and managed just two completions on four attempts. He threw two interceptions and finished the game with just seventeen yards

But the shock of the evening for Coach Riley was not the performance of any particular player, but rather the reaction of the crowd when veteran, Don Jonas stepped out on the field.

The former Shenley winner was booed by the hometown crowd of 16,000 near the end of second quarter before he even touched the ball. The crowd's anger only intensified and grew louder when his first pass attempt was intercepted.

Following the game, the shocked Coach Riley was quoted as saying, "I couldn't believe it. I guess he'll have to gain 'em back." Meanwhile, Brock had received nothing but cheers.

Many believed Jonas was washed up at the age of thirty-six, while others felt the crowd's reaction had been because of the players' strike.

Coach Riley also had some concerns with Jonas's age and stated that he would have no hesitation in using Brock. "I've never seen a young quarterback with more poise than Brock has," Riley was quoted.

D.C. Nobles had appeared confused in the game and had difficulty with exchanges from the center. The following day, after the loss, he was released, leaving Jonas, Brock and Pharr as the team's quarterbacks going into the future.

When questioned by the media about his line-up a few days later, Riley still insisted he "would have no hesitation in naming Brock as the number one quarterback. He has exceptional ability, but for no other reason, we have to go with seniority, we've got to go with experience, especially at the quarterback position."

In the second pre-season game against Toronto, Jonas looked impressive in the first half throwing seven passes on eleven attempts for one-hundred and twenty-five yards and one interception. Brock struggled at his time behind center, completing just three passes for forty yards on seven attempts.

In a 30-15 win against Saskatchewan, Jonas would go almost the whole distance, leaving Brock just over two minutes in the fourth quarter.

In their last pre-season game, the Ottawa Rough Riders held the Bombers to a 27-16 loss. Winnipeg had made it respectable on the scoreboard with two last minute touchdowns by Brock.

As expected, Jonas was assigned the starting position for the team's first regular season game and the result was a 29-22 loss against the B.C. Lions.

In the following week, in a rematch against the same B.C. Lions, Brock saw limited playing time, going in to relieve the struggling Jonas during the fourth quarter. The result was another loss of 26-6.

With a 0-2 record, Coach Riley continued putting his faith in his number one quarterback. Jonas was set to start against the Saskatchewan Roughriders in the next game, but Riley didn't deny he would use Brock if the situation called for relief again.

And by the fourth quarter, the situation did warrant relief. Brock was sent in with the Roughriders leading the game 24-6, but it was too little, too late. The Blue Bombers left Regina with a 24-13 loss and a season record of 0-3.

On August 21, it seemed that things may be turning around for the Blue Bombers when they earned a win against the Toronto Argonauts. Jonas went the distance in an impressive display of leadership and control on the field. Angered by previous media reports, Jonas stated after the game in an interview, "There were a lot of reasons why this football team wasn't winning, not just Don Jonas."

The difference in that game was that the coaches had called every play from the sideline, but despite the team's win, Jonas was still not happy. "Of course I don't like it," he was quoted. "But how can I argue about the system. We won. It's good to get the monkey off our backs. Now if I can get just get management off mine."

The next two games earned the team victories against the Calgary Stampeders and the Saskatchewan Roughriders. It seemed that the Blue Bombers had finally found their stride with Jonas leading the way. Brock had been left on the sideline, seeing limited time on the field.

But immediately after the Saskatchewan win, in a move that shocked the team and the league, it was announced that Don Jonas had been traded to the Hamilton Tiger-Cats for younger, veteran quarterback, Chuck Ealey.

"The trade was a complete surprise to everybody on the team," recalled Brock. "We had just come off a three-game winning streak. Winning that game in Regina and being told in the airport that Don was traded... , it was total surprise to everyone."

Coach Riley had wanted a change and he got it.

It was rumored that Chuck Ealey was not happy with his situation in Hamilton. It began in the off-season when

Ealey and a few other players had claimed they had signed their contracts under the 14 game season agreement. With the league now in a 16 game schedule, they wanted to renegotiate extra compensation for the added games. The resulting trade was a shock to Ealey because he had heard the news over the radio like everyone else.

Chuck Ealey had burst onto the CFL scene in 1972 with the Hamilton Tiger-Cats and in his first season had been named the Outstanding Rookie in the CFL. Ealey completed 58.4% of his passes for 2,573 yards and 22 touchdowns. He had also led the Tiger-Cats to a Grey Cup win over the Saskatchewan Roughriders in his rookie season.

In 1973, Ealey put up similar stats, completing 58.6% of his passes for 2,312 yards. Ealey was not only a threat in the air, but also on the ground. He rushed for 515 yards in his rookie season and 687 yards in his second year. In 1974, however, things soured for Ealey as he got off to slow start throwing eight interceptions and only two touchdown passes.

Jonas took the trade in stride and agreed to report to Hamilton in the following days. He had outside commitments to clear up and couldn't leave immediately. Jonas had been a sport's consultant at Eaton's Department Store and also ran his own travel agency.

Ealey, on the other hand, arrived almost immediately, giving him just four days to prepare for the Blue Bombers' next game against Edmonton. But even with the veteran's experience, Riley chose Brock to start the September 7 game, shocking Edmonton's coach, Ray Jauch. "We're trying to find this guy on film to see how good he is."

No one seemed to know how good Brock was. Despite his glowing testimonies from the coaching staff, he had only been called in to mop up the disasters and that isn't easy.

"It was tough," said Brock. "I wasn't playing much and still didn't fully understand defences."

"I know I had a pretty good pre-season," he said. "But I had hurt my throwing shoulder in the last pre-season game. This was the same shoulder that I had hurt in the

first game of the 1973 season with Jacksonville State, so it
wasn't a new injury. But I remember Tommy Pharr telling
me to not say anything to anybody because there was a
possibility that if they thought you were hurt, you'd be
released. And especially a quarterback who had hurt his
throwing shoulder and was considered to be just a back-
up."

Ralph Brock would start his first professional game
against the Edmonton Eskimos and he paid the price. The
young quarterback was beaten down by the Eskimos
defence. He was sacked five times and was only able to
move the ball 87 yards on the ground and 57 yards in the
air.

Ealey was sent in to rescue the team, but he received
the same treatment, getting sacked twice on the eight plays
he called. The final result was 24-2 loss.

"I was terrible in that game," Brock recalls. "I got killed
from all the hits because I had no clue what I was doing."

The rest of the season continued to have its ups and
downs for the Blue Bombers. Ealey remained the starting
quarterback while Brock watched from the sidelines for the
most part. The Blue Bombers finished the year with a
dismal 8-8 record and finished fourth in the Western
Conference.

"After that Edmonton game, I think that was about it
for the 1974 season for me," said Brock. "I had completed
all of 12 passes in 27 attempts for 176 yards. I didn't throw
for any touchdowns, but did throw two interceptions."

"It was kind of a tough first year, but I liked Winnipeg.
It was a different world from Birmingham, but we enjoyed
it at times that first year."

"I had signed a one-year contract and I guess the club
had an option to keep me for another year at the same
price. I hadn't played much, but I started to learn what it
was going to take to become good quarterback in
professional football. I had a much better understanding of
the game and knew a little more about defences."

"But that trade really opened my eyes to professional
football," said Brock. "Trading a guy like Don who had just
won three consecutive games, a guy that has been an MOP

in the league and had completely turned the Blue Bombers around after some horrible years, kind of shook me up. I totally did not understand it."

"The only thing I knew was they were getting a much younger quarterback in Ealey, who had won a Grey Cup. And to me, that meant they didn't think very much of me."

"I knew I had to get stronger and bigger to handle the punishment of a 16 game season if I was ever going to become a starting quarterback. Don Jonas had been traded for a much younger quarterback and there was no waiting in the wings now. If I was going to make it as a professional quarterback, then I was going to have to start from scratch and dedicate myself to becoming the hardest working athlete ever."

Chapter Seven

"Nobody was going to outwork me in the off-season," recalls Brock. "I had made up my mind that I was going to be the quarterback for the Winnipeg Blue Bombers and I was determined to do whatever it took."

After a mediocre rookie season because of limited playing opportunities and the addition of a veteran quarterback, it's hard to imagine how Ralph Brock could have maintained such an optimistic attitude about his future with the Blue Bombers. He had reported to his first professional training camp as a young 23 year-old understudy to a 36 year-old veteran. Halfway through the season, the 36 year old was replaced by a 26 year-old veteran who had already had a taste of being a champion and was carrying the hopes of the team on his shoulders.

"I'll admit I didn't feel very good after the Jonas trade," said Brock. "I felt I had a chance to take over when Don left, then, all of a sudden the future seemed a long way off."

It certainly didn't help pad Brock's resume when his first professional career start against the Edmonton Eskimos turned into a total disaster. No one would have blamed him if he had of just walked away from the game entirely after the beat down he had experienced. But then again, no one knew who Ralph Brock really was.

"That off-season was when I got into serious weight lifting and working out," said Brock. While other players spent the off-season working to make ends meet, Brock focused on improving himself. "I felt my job in the off-season was to try to get better as a player and a quarterback. I seldom took a day off from weight workouts and running and throwing exercises."

He worked weights for the first time in his career and did weighted ball throws in a self-designed program. "I made three different weighted balls by putting pellets and BBs inside of a plastic whiffle ball and wrapping it with electrical tape. I made a 4 pound, a 3 pound ball and a 2 pound. I had a thick rubber mat that I nailed between two trees in my backyard. The mat was high enough so that I could throw the balls and release them at different angles. I could make throws as if I would have to drill the ball or if I were throwing long passes. After throwing the ball into the rubber mat, it would just drop down and I would catch it, ready to throw again."

"The workout on the weighted ball throws was strictly for the off-season," he explained. "I would start by throwing the 4 pound ball two to three hundred times a day for a month. Then I would drop down to the 3 pound ball and do the same thing for a month. Then on third month, I would drop to the 2 pound ball, again throwing two to three hundred throws a day. By dropping from the four pound ball to the two over a three month period, I was getting faster and faster arm speed."

"After the weighted ball throws, I had a weighted football which weighed about a pound and a half and I would throw that for two to three weeks. By the time I got to the regular football which weighs a little under a pound, I had tremendous arm speed."

"I also studied and used the weight lifting workouts of the top javelin throwers in the world."

The intense regime not only improved his physical state, but gave his confidence a boost as well.

"I had gained about 10 lb of upper body strength and was feeling stronger than I had ever been in my life," said Brock. "Doing all those throwing exercises put my arm in the best condition ever. I had a great arm before that, but now I had a rocket from doing all the throwing exercises."

"I called Earl Lunsford during that off-season feeling pretty confident because I was getting bigger and stronger," said Brock. "I told Earl that I wanted a three year guaranteed contract for something like $30,000 a year. He must have thought I had lost my mind after doing absolutely nothing on the field the year before. I looked terrible in the only game I had played in and now I was asking for a three-year guaranteed contract? He must have laughed his ass off after that call."

But the Blue Bombers' general manager wasn't laughing. "He told me that he would sign me to another year with a $2,000 raise and that I was lucky to get that."

"I really had no intention of going anywhere else. We liked Winnipeg and Earl was right, I was lucky to have gotten even that deal."

The Winnipeg Blue Bombers' opened their 1975 Training Camp in early June with four quarterbacks; the veteran, Chuck Ealey, sophomore back-up, Ralph Brock, Kelly Cochrane from 1974 and newcomer, J.C. Smith.

"When Brock showed up to camp that year, I thought he was a linebacker," recalls former CKY sports reporter, Peter Young. "His arms were massive. And you could tell he had a whole new sense of confidence around him. He was still quiet and very polite when the media was around him. But he was definitely focused."

Lunsford and Riley had also brought in a newcomer, J.C. Smith. "In 1974, I was released by the Oakland Raiders from the NFL and the Chicago Fire from the WFL," said J.C. Smith. "Both teams had been blessed with seasoned quarterbacks; Ken "The Snake" Stabler in Oakland and NFL veteran Virgil Carter in Chicago."

"Earl Lunsford had solid NFL and WFL contacts and had received a positive evaluation of my quarterbacking ability from both teams. I contacted him about the status of Blue Bomber quarterbacks and was told that Chuck Ealey was the number one Blue Bombers' quarterback. His back-up was Ralph Brock, a rookie from Jacksonville State. Lunsford said he wasn't certain what the future held for Ralph Brock in 1975."

"Bud Riley, the head coach believed in the importance of bringing the quarterbacks into camp a few days early to familiarize them with the team's system and offensive strategy," said Smith. "I walked onto the practice-field next to the Winnipeg Stadium and saw the coaches. Chuck

Ealey and second-year invite Kelly Cochran from Tampa were warming-up along with Brock."

"Quarterbacks constantly evaluate each other in regards to their throwing motion and mechanics. When I saw Brock's first throw, it was easy to see that his delivery was compact, smooth, and effortless with plenty of velocity. I had never seen such a tight spiral. The ball actually whistled through the air like a projectile."

"When I first met him," Smith continued. "I was amazed when observing his arm strength and his ability to throw the deep ball. All of us threw the long ball when we had a chance, but nobody threw better than Brock."

"That's how the slogan, 'When in doubt, air it out" came from. The fastest way to score in football is the long pass for a touchdown. We wanted to use the long ball as a weapon to destroy the defence."

"That was just some silly saying that us quarterbacks came up with in 1975," said Brock. "We loved to throw the football deep. It came from a pass route that Bud Riley had in his offence, where we had a quick hot throw if a receiver was open and a deep post route over the top. Of course all the quarterbacks loved to throw the ball deep, especially me."

"One day in practice, I threw the post route several times and missed the receiver. Bud yelled out, 'Throw the hot! Throw the hot!' So, after practice, J.C. came up with the goofy saying, 'When in doubt, air it out.'"

Cochrane was an early departure, lasting just a few days in camp, while the three remaining quarterbacks performed well. Ealey still held the number one spot, followed by Brock and Smith in that order. Coach Riley had said numerous times that Brock had certainly matured as a player.

During the team's first pre-season game, the entire quarterback trio saw game action against the Saskatchewan Roughriders, but it was Brock who brought the team alive in the third quarter after the team was down 8-6. In less than seven minutes, Brock had two touchdowns on the board, giving the Blue Bombers a 20-8 lead. By the end of the game, the Blue Bombers had won, 41-8.

But the following week, against the Toronto Argonauts, things seemed to go a bit sideways. In the fourth quarter, Brock had the team moving and it seemed the Blue Bombers were going to increase their one point lead. But the Argonauts defence came alive and put the heat on Brock, causing losses of 11 and 12 yards and a Brock fumble. He finished the game 0-4 with one interception and let the Argonauts walk away with a 15-14 win.

The following day, the Blue Bombers announced the release of J.C. Smith. Riley had said his development was equal to Brock's in his rookie year, but Brock had improved so much in the off-season that the rookie's departure was evident.

The Blue Bombers would eventually finish the 1975 pre-season with a 1-3 record. Two days before their regular season opener against the B.C. Lions, Bud Riley announced that Chuck Ealey had maintained his status as the team's number one quarterback. He had given serious consideration to starting Brock after his impressive pre-season performance, but felt Ealey deserved the opportunity to start.

"Ealey's our number one man," Riley was quoted as saying. "And he deserves to start. But I won't hesitate to get Brock in there if the situation calls for it."

In the team's regular season opener against the Lions, the only on-field time Brock had was to hold the ball for four field goals and during a faked field goal attempt where he threw an incomplete pass deep down field.

Ealey handled the win against the Lions, 17-9, but suffered an injury the following week in a 28-22 loss against Edmonton.

The following week, in a return battle against Edmonton, Brock was forced to take over midway through the second quarter when Ealey's injury wouldn't allow him to plant his right foot to throw. Brock would complete just 10 of the 25 passes he threw, but his timing was perfect. Two of his completions were caught by receiver, Tom Scott, for touchdowns, giving the Blue Bombers the 17-16 win.

Brock got the nod against the Calgary Stampeders and led the Blue Bombers to an 18-15 win in the next game. He completed just eight passes and ran the ball 38 yards, but his impressive performance made it clear that he had become the Blue Bombers number one quarterback. Chuck Ealey, now number two, would have to work his way back and prove he deserved to be anything else.

Starting against the Saskatchewan Roughriders, Brock had a big night. He completed 13 of the 22 passes he threw and had a six-yard average when running the ball. His passing accounted for 137 yards and his running added 24 more which meant he contributed 161 yards of the Blue Bombers 185 in total offence.

But despite his performance, the Ron Lancaster Roughriders were on the winning side of the game; 20-13.

Riley made the decision to start Ealey in the next game against Calgary. After a slow start, the Blue Bombers blocked a kick and recovered the ball which seemed to fire up the team. Ealey ran the ball 11 times for 82 yards. Four of his runs produced key first downs for the team and they went on to beat the Stampeders 25-22.

In a Labour Day match-up against the Roughriders, the Blue Bombers dominated the football. They had possession of the ball almost twice as long as Saskatchewan. Under the leadership of Ealey, they seemed to have all facets of their attack working as they marched up and down the field. But in the final analysis of the game, it was a case of too much Ron Lancaster once again and the Blue Bombers lost 27-23.

Five days later, the Blue Bombers faced the B.C. Lions at Empire Stadium, in Vancouver. Winnipeg led 9-1 at the half on three field goals by Bernie Ruoff while the Lions had managed just four first downs. But in the second half, Lion's veteran quarterback, Peter Liske brought the Empire Stadium crowd of 17,000 to their feet by throwing three touchdown passes, giving the Lions and their new head coach, Cal Murphy, their first victory.

The following week was an embarrassing 15-1 loss against the same B.C. Lions. Ealey was sacked twice in the first half. Brock was sent in to relieve the veteran in the third quarter, but didn't fare much better. He threw an interception that was taken back for a touchdown and was sacked three times. The Blue Bombers ran just 30 plays from scrimmage compared to the Lions' 62.

"We had now lost three games in a row and we seemed to be getting worse each game," said Brock. "On Monday, after that third loss, Bud Riley came in to the locker room holding everyone's game cheque and placed them all on a table in the center of the room. He lectured everyone about how we were stealing money from the team because of how bad we were playing. I think he said something to the effect that if anyone thought they were playing well enough to earn their game cheque, they could come and get it. I don't think anyone moved while Bud stood there. But I can guarantee you, after he left the room, everyone picked up their cheques."

Riley's locker room lecture seemed to have an effect on the team. Against the Hamilton Tiger-Cats the following week, Ealey led the Blue Bombers to a 34-32 win.

"We had a two-game swing in the East up next where we played in Toronto on the Friday night and then Montreal on Monday," said Brock. "Our tenth game of the season was against the Argonauts in Toronto. Chuck started the game, but we weren't doing very well. Coach Riley put me in to start the second half and we came back to tie the game, 21-21."

Brock had taken control of the game and it appeared that Riley, frustrated, had given up on Ealey and It was time for him to make a move that some people had said should have been done earlier in the season.

"We got to Montreal and I remember Bud Riley calling my room. He told me to come to his room. He said we needed to talk," said Brock. "And that's when he told me that the starting quarterback job was mine to keep going forward. That meant as long as I played well, I would keep the starting quarterback job."

"We went on to beat Montreal, 26-21. I think I had over 300 yards passing and threw a couple of touchdowns against a very good Montreal defence. They went to the Grey Cup that year."

The Alouettes had spent their time preparing for Chuck Ealey to play quarterback for the Blue Bombers, not Brock. They didn't even know Brock's first name was Ralph.

After the Montreal game, the Winnipeg Tribune's Jack Matheson wrote,

"I haven't seen anybody throw a football like that for Winnipeg since Indian Jack was among us, and if you don't want to take my word for it you might want to get in touch with Kenny Ploen, who won more football games than any other Winnipeg quarterback, living or dead. K.P. just couldn't stop shaking his head, and the superlatives just kept coming."

In a surprising move, the Blue Bombers brought in a new quarterback, Harry Knight, for a five day trial. Knight, a dropback passer, had been drafted by the Oakland Raiders and had been recently released from the NFL team.

In the Blue Bombers' next game, despite a 20-14 loss against the Roughriders, Brock was impressive. Trailing by 13 points with six minutes left in the game, Brock moved the ball half the field for a touchdown in just six plays. He then moved 105 yards in eight plays and came within four yards of the winning score.

The fact that he coughed up the ball with 28 seconds left in the game didn't seem to faze anyone. All they knew was that Brock had completed 12 of 13 passes under severe pressure from the relentless Saskatchewan defence.

With Brock having a firm grip on the number one spot, Chuck Ealey was now expendable. On October 14, Ealey was traded to the Toronto Argonauts. Harry Knight had impressed Riley with his abilities and was signed as Brock's understudy. Riley knew he was on the right track and had to act fast when the New York Jets and L.A. Rams had starting inquiring about Knight's availability.

"We played Ottawa in a 21-21 tie game after that," said Brock. "I had my first 400 yard passing game, throwing four touchdown passes against Edmonton a couple of weeks later in the snow, but we lost 48 to 41. I think we had scored only 25 points or better twice that whole season until I became the starter. Then in the last five games of the season, with me starting, we scored 25 or better four times. But we still only had a record of 1-3-1.

But at the end of the regular season, Brock had taken the Blue Bombers to a season record of 6-8-2, placing them in third place in the Western Conference and enough to put them in the Western play-offs.

"We played Saskatchewan in the semi-final game in Regina," said Brock. "Unfortunately, we got walloped pretty good, 42-24, by Ronnie Lancaster and George Reed and a defence that intercepted four of my passes. I was so pissed off after I threw the fourth interception that I made a beeline to try to make the tackle myself. Out of nowhere came Bill Baker, the great Hall of Fame defensive end. I have never been hit so hard in my career. Well, that taught me a lesson about trying to make tackles after an interception. Bill Baker was one of the best defensive players that I've ever played against."

At the end of the game, there was no doubt that Roughriders quarterback, Ron Lancaster, shared the star status with his team's defence. Their relentless attack on Brock threw the entire Blue Bomber offence off balance and it seemed like they wouldn't stop coming.

"Even with that loss, I think I had established myself as the starting quarterback for the Winnipeg Blue Bombers in the future."

"After I became the starter, the number of passes each game went up because I was calling the plays," said Brock. "I remember the Hogs, the offensive line of Bob Swift, Chuck Liebrock, Bill Frank, Chuck Harrison, Butch Norman and Buddy Brown would sometimes suggest to our offensive line coach, Joe Faragalli, that we should be running the football more. To my surprise, Joe responded by telling them to just run the play that I called."

"After that, no one from the offensive line ever came to me and told me what to do again. I think they respected the toughness and confidence that I had started to show on and off the field."

Two days after the Saskatchewan play-off loss, Earl Lunsford, the Blue Bomber's general manager, made an announcement from the Hotel Fort Garry. Bud Riley had agreed to a new two year contract with the team.

Riley, who was about to celebrate his 50th birthday, was 8-8, in his first year as the Blue Bombers head coach. In 1975, the Blue Bombers had made the playoffs at 6-8-2.

"There no question in our minds that we've made progress with Bud," said Lunsford in front of the media. "When you bring in a new coach, you're giving him a mandate to begin rebuilding."

"We had problems last year that carried through Don Jonas and Chuck Ealey," said Riley at the same press conference. "But we finally began solving the problem with the emergence of Brock."

"And I predict, we'll see a greatly improved Ralph Brock in '76," said Riley.

Brock, on his way back home to Birmingham was aware of Riley's comments. "All that did was made me want to work harder to get better as a quarterback because this was my team now."

Chapter Eight

Going into the '76 season, despite the fact that they had won just six regular season games in the 1975 season, the Winnipeg Blue Bombers were being touted by some as the team to watch. George Brancato, the head coach of the Ottawa Rough Riders, was reported as saying, "Look out for this team. They're much better than their 1975 record indicates." And John Payne from the Saskatchewan Roughriders was also noted as saying, "Winnipeg is the team which may surprise everyone."

Football is obviously a team sport, but since the beginning, the weight of a team's success can sometimes fall at the feet of one or two key players. That responsibility can be earned, assigned or even implied, with or without the player's consent. Before the last whistle had blown to end the Blue Bombers' 1975 season, the responsibility for the Winnipeg team's future was already being placed on the shoulders of a young Ralph Brock. At the time, some of that made perfect sense. After all, age and experience shouldn't really matter when you've earned the number one starting quarterback position of a professional football team. Or should it?

What most people failed to understand was that going into that 1976 season, Ralph Brock was still technically a rookie starter. The 24 year-old was just eighteen months out of a small American college with very little actual game experience. He had openly admitted that the Canadian game was still a bit confusing for him and he still was learning how to read defences.

Growing up, Brock had lived in the same neighbourhood for most of his life, and played with the same friends and familiar faces since elementary school. Now he was now expected to lead a group of unfamiliar men, in a foreign city and country to a place in history. Ralph Brock, inexperienced and still a little naive, felt the weight of that responsibility and embraced it.

Most professional coaches will tell you that it takes a quarterback at least four years to achieve a level of maturity and knowledge to successfully carry a team. Ron Lancaster, the best in the league at that time, had come into the CFL in 1959, but he never really made it until 1964. And even then, he hadn't come up a winner until 1966. Tom Wilkinson had also been around the league for a long time with a variety of teams before he made it to that level.

Jack Matheson once wrote "Learning to play quarterback in the pros can take as long as learning to be a surgeon." In 1976, Ralph Brock was still an intern when it came to leading a team, reading defences and understanding the flow of the game.

When he did make it on the field in 1975, he definitely made an impression. But he had been sacked twenty-nine times in that one season. By comparison, Saskatchewan's Ron Lancaster was sacked just nine times while Edmonton's two quarterbacks, Tom Wilkinson and Bruce Lemmerman were sacked a total of just ten times.

"Since that was going to be my first full year as a starter in professional football, I knew there were certain things I needed to improve on," said Brock. "Number one was my completion percentage which was terrible in '75. I knew I really had to start making better decisions on the field."

In 1975, the Blue Bombers had averaged 291 yards per game under Chuck Ealey. In the five games under Brock, they averaged 384 yards per game.

"I knew we were going to continue to run the same offence, so I spent a lot of time on the playbook studying my reads and decision making. I think in '75 there were too many times when I went for the deep ball more than I should have. I should have just dumped the ball off for a completion instead of trying to always make the big play."

The results from Brock's self-designed post season work-outs and conditioning had made a huge difference in the young quarterback when he first appeared at the '75 training camping, so it made sense to repeat the same when he returned home to Birmingham.

"I went back to my lifting workouts and throwing weighted balls," said Brock. "But I had a lot more intensity and determination this time. I developed drills to work on my footwork and my dropbacks. I ran three to four miles a day and played in a community basketball league. I also played tennis and golfed at least once a week."

"It's hard for people to fully understand and appreciate exactly how dedicated he was during the off-season," said long-time friend, Larry "Snapper" Lancaster.

"I first met him when he was sixteen or seventeen," recalls Snapper. "I was a postman for 42 years and his neighbourhood was on my route. I kept hearing about this kid from Jones Valley High who could throw the ball like a bullet. One day I saw a group of kids playing on the street and a ball just flew through the air. I figured that was the kid everyone was talking about."

In a very short time, and despite their eight year age difference, Brock and Lancaster became inseparable for many years. "Every night he would call and say, 'Hey Snap, let's go throw.' My wife wasn't too happy about it, but I'd go anyway."

"In the off seasons, during his time with the Blue Bombers, he had two trees in his backyard that were eight to ten feet apart," said Lancaster. "He stretched a thick rubber tarp out between them and throw a 20 pound weight at with his right hand. The weight would bounce back and he'd catch it with his left hand. He would do that for hours every day. Sometimes he'd throw it 400 times."

"Some days we'd go down to the Jones Valley field. He would line up on the goal line and I'd stand at the 35," said Snapper. "He'd tap the ball and I'd just go. He'd take his three step drop and then launch it right in my arms. Here's the thing about his passes; he would throw them so you couldn't miss."

"One day, someone came out and asked how far he could throw. 'Let's see,' he said. We did that same drill, but instead of starting at the 35, he told me to go to mid field. I saw him tap the ball then ran straight down the sideline. When the ball landed in my arms, I stopped and looked down. It was a 95 yard throw."

"I've seen a lot of athletes in my time," said Snapper. "But his commitment and dedication to being the best he could be was something I've never seen and I'll never forget," said Lancaster. "All he talked about was his team and being the best he could be."

"In that off-season, I focused on improving my game because I wanted to be the best. I could feel the faith the Blue Bombers had in me," he said. "I was ready to spend six months away from home for my team for the next number of years. After that season, I had a little more confidence in asking them for a long-term commitment and more money. I felt that was only fair."

"We had bought a house in Birmingham that year and were expecting our first child," said Brock. "A new contract brought me a bit more security and helped take some of the pressure off so I could focus on the seasons ahead. Eventually, we agreed to a three year contract for $160,000."

The new contract guaranteed Brock $48,000 a year and placed him among the highest paid players in the league. The average salary on the Winnipeg Blue Bombers at that time was $24,000.

"I think sometimes people in Winnipeg thought of me as a Birmingham quarterback that just played in Winnipeg," said Brock. "But even going back to that second meeting with Bud Riley in 1974, in my heart and mind, I was a Winnipeg Blue Bomber quarterback who just happened to live in Birmingham."

Just like in the previous season, Coach Bud Riley stuck with his routine and assembled the quarterbacks early. In the off-season, Riley had decided he wanted another look at J.C. Smith and he was brought back into camp. Brock, Knight and Smith gathered a week ahead of the official training camp, three weeks ahead of the first pre-season game and six weeks ahead of the season opener.

The trio would spend their days inside the football club's meeting room studying the offensive scheme and playbook before adjourning to the field at 4:30 in the afternoon.

In that early week, the media would get their pre-season look at Brock and the other two throwing the football outside the Maroons Road office. Just a few days in, Jack Matheson wrote his opening piece in the Winnipeg Tribune calling Brock a "Greek God" and joked about him getting time off during the season to compete in the Mr. Manitoba competition at the annual Red River Exhibition.

"It was nice to be considered number one," said Brock. "It was good to come back knowing I had a job and now all I wanted to do was to win a bunch of games for the Blue Bombers."

He was determined and convinced that 1976 was going to be his year and that the only role Harry Knight and J.C. Smith would have was to sit back and watch.

"It was basically the same offence as the year before," said Brock. "I understood the plays so all we really had to do was focus more on executing them as a team."

On June 13, 1976, nineteen veterans and twenty-four rookies reported to St John's Ravenscourt School for the opening of the Blue Bomber's training camp. The first drill started that evening, then moved to three-a –day workouts the following day.

The schedule was rigid with a 7:30am breakfast, 9:00am workout on the field, a noon lunch break, a 3:00pm on-field practice, 6:00pm dinner and 8:00pm on-field meetings.

On June 21, Coach Riley put his offence to the test in a special exercise. Each quarterback had just ten plays to move the ball downfield against the defence. The name of the game was to move the ball as far as they could and it was their game to call until they'd made four consecutive first downs, or lost the ball by interception or fumble or the sequence just ran out gas. No one was really surprised when Brock out performed them all.

In the team's first pre-season game against Calgary, Brock played the first twenty minutes, giving Knight and Smith some play action. The three quarterbacks combined for 492 yards in total offence, winning 39-27.

In his twenty minutes, Brock was 13-9-1 for 194 yards. Knight was 10-5-0 for 129 yards while Smith's night was 2-1 for just 20 yards. There was no question that Ralph Brock was Blue Bombers' number one quarterback.

One of the most obvious changes that had been observed in the '76 offence was the team's sprint series offence. Riley had originally designed the scheme for the running ability of Chuck Ealey, but it was Brock who actually perfected it.

Properly executed, the sprint series kept defences from committing longer than most offensive schemes. It was designed to allow Ealey to roll out wide and run the ball. But Brock had the ability to roll out and then run or pass, which kept the defence guessing until it was too late for them to react.

Next up in the pre-season schedule was the Hamilton Tiger-Cats. Brock went 12-6-1 for 127 yards, Smith was 5-2 for 50 yards and Knight finished the game 9-6 for 112 yards. But despite the 38-3 win against the Tiger-Cats, Brock was not satisfied with his consistency in the game. "I was still not where I wanted to be," he said.

J.C. Smith was released on July 8. He never really had a chance to make the team as some around the league were saying Brock and Knight may be the best quarterback set in the CFL's pre-season. Smith, being a left hander never showed much to Coach Riley in camp. According to Riley's comments to the media, he kept putting more pressure on himself and the result was he couldn't spot the open receivers and was inclined to throw late and wild.

In the next pre-season matchup, a 32-30 loss to Edmonton, Brock was sacked four times, but still managed to finish with a record of 23-14 for 183 yards. Harry Knight saw limited time on the field, going 4-2-1 for just 20 yards.

In their final pre-season game against B.C., the Lions' defence was suffocating. On paper, the Lions recorded just two official sacks, but it was worse than the numbers showed. Brock took a terrible beating and his final stats for the game were a dismal 30-12-2 for 174 yards in the 24-19 loss.

But by the time the pre-season was over, it was clear that the 1976 Winnipeg Blue Bombers were loaded with talent. With Brock at quarterback, backed-up by Knight, they also had Steve Beaird and Jim Washington at running back. Mark McDonald was the out wide and Tommy Scott and Gord Paterson were set at wingback. Bob LaRose was at flanker behind Bob Swift with Chuck Liebrock, Buddy Brown, Butch Norman and Bill Frank on the offensive line. Defensively, Jim Heighton and Elton Brown were the ends, while Dave Knechtel and Don Hubbard were at tackle in the front four. Harry Walters, Bob Toogood and John Babinecz were the linebacker corp and Merv Walker, Chuck Wills, Brian Herosian, Lee Benard and Vince Phason stood strong in the secondary. The kicker, Bernie Ruoff was also considered a real weapon for the team.

The regular season opener against the Toronto Argonauts was being billed as Brock vs Ealey. The former teammates were set to meet each other on July 22. But unfortunately both quarterbacks were pulled by their respective coaches in the third quarter of the game for their lack of production and failing to move the ball. Brock was able to return later in the game to work off some of his frustrations, but the final outcome was still a disappointing 22-16 loss for the Blue Bombers.

The following week against the Ottawa Rough Riders, Brock was sacked six times for losses of 60 yards, but he still managed to throw a 40 yard and a 12 yard touchdown pass. He completed 16 of 30 attempts for 275 yards, but as a team, they lost, 38-27. The Blue Bombers had also lost their starting running back, Steve Beaird, on the first play of the game with badly bruised ribs.

Things started to look promising on August 3 when Brock seemed to have found his rhythm and the Blue Bombers hammered the Calgary Stampeders, 49-3. He completed 13 of 22 passes to Bob LaRose, Tom Scott and Jim Washington.

Then came the reigning Grey Cup Champions, the Edmonton Eskimos. In the late 70's the Eskimos always seemed to find a way to rain on the Blue Bombers' parade, but on August 10, they trailed the Blue Bombers for most of the game. In the fourth quarter with their unbeaten status in serious jeopardy, quarterback Bruce Lemmerman made a miraculous effort to tie the game allowing Dave Cutler to kick the winning point in a tight 31-30 showdown.

Throughout the Edmonton game, Brock continued his tendency to throw deep. He launched textbook bombs to Mark McDonald and Tom Scott, but it was the throws that didn't connect that had Coach Riley frustrated. He admitted he would have liked to see Brock throw more short hooks. But according to the statistics, Brock's completed passes had averaged 13 yards, the same as Ron Lancaster's and only one yard longer than Tom Wilkinson.

Six days later, in Vancouver, the Blue Bombers took an early lead against the B.C. Lions. In the second quarter, Brock used a fake field goal to connect with running back, Richard Crump for 33 yards. But at the B.C. 12 yard line, on second down, Brock was swallowed up by the BC defence and the team had to settle for a field goal. It had been a game of defences and the Lions had proven better at it than the Blue Bombers, beating them, 22-14.

At that point in the season, the Blue Bombers were 1-4, but the scoreboard numbers didn't exactly tell the tale of the team. They had averaged 27 points per game and had thrown more passes than any other team in the league. Brock had thrown 158 passes with only five interceptions, an impressive statistic. For Edmonton, Tom Wilkinson and Bruce Lemmerman combined had thrown 158 passes and had 12 picked off. The Blue Bombers had scored 15 touchdowns while only two other teams in the league had scored more.

But what the statistics did not show was that the problem may not have been just the quarterback; it was the men that were supposed to be protecting him. Brock had been sacked for 18 losses in the five games, a league high. Some were again complaining that the team was too pass oriented, but the offence had thrown 158 passes and rushed 132 times, a normal pass-run ratio in the league at the time.

In football, passes move the ball almost twice as fast as runs. The Blue Bombers had 1,357 yards in passing compared to 766 in rushing; proving that going in the air was the easiest and quickest way to put points on the board. The longest pass in the league at that point in the season was a 97 yard bomb from Brock to Tom Scott.

But the only numbers that really mattered was their dismal 1-4 record. As a result, veteran captains, Bob Swift and Bill Frank called a players-only meeting prior to the next game.

"I had never been involved in a player's only meeting before," said Brock. "I wasn't one of those guys that were into these meetings because a lot of times they just become a blame game between the offence and defence. I believed in just working hard on improving one's self and trying to do what the coaches were asking of us as a team."

"But this one was different. It wasn't a blame game. They talked about how we had a good team and it was on all of us to pull together to get it right or there were going to be changes made. They gave other players a chance to have their say, but I don't recall exactly what was said or who said it. I know I didn't say anything because I felt confident that we had a good team and I felt confident in our offence."

"I knew we were a fairly young team with Butch Norman and Buddy Brown being new offensive lineman and obviously with me being the new starting quarterback," said Brock. "But I guess the meeting worked out okay because we started winning."

In Saskatchewan the next week, the defence did an outstanding job shutting Ron Lancaster down. Offensively, with just over a minute to play, Brock led the Blue Bombers down the field with a purpose. On a roll right, he hit Bob LaRose from the five line yard for the only touchdown of the night, giving the team a 13-12 victory. Brock was sacked just once and was given all kinds of time to set up and do his thing. He ended the night 24-38 for 264 yards with four interceptions, but Lancaster finished with 21-36 for 240 yards and five interceptions.

Against Calgary, they relied on the Big Play from Brock's arm once again. The offence couldn't establish a running game so Brock used the bomb and that was all they needed. He threw a 47 yard touchdown pass to Tom Scott in the second quarter and a 32 yarder to the same receiver in the fourth to beat Calgary, 29-20.

On September 2, while the team celebrated their two game winning streak and prepared for the next game against Hamilton, Ralph and Kathy Brock celebrated the birth of their first daughter, Melanie Michelle at Winnipeg's Health Sciences Centre.

But four days later, the new father and his receivers were not at their best in Hamilton. Brock seemed impatient and was once again prone to throwing for the big play. But that only works if the passer and receiver are on the same page and able to connect. The whole night was a disappointing display of dropped balls and rushed plays that led to a Bombers' defeat of 17-15 against the Tiger Cats.

By mid-season, the Blue Bombers were 3-5 and stuck in fourth place in the Western Conference. They had beaten the first place Roughriders and had played competitively against the Edmonton Eskimos. Coach Riley blamed the team's record on inconsistency and their lack of execution on the field. But he was still satisfied with his young quarterback and was confident that he would improve over time.

It was around that time the Winnipeg Tribune's Jack Matheson wrote,

"The passing game is adequate. Ralph Brock, the Birmingham Rifle, is taking longer to play Moses than he was supposed to, but there isn't any doubt he'll be worth waiting for. Maturity will bring a little more patience and Brock will be happy to throw short four times to Scott and Patterson instead of blowing the whole wad on a 50 yarder to nobody."

Against the B.C. Lions, a must win game for the Blue Bombers, Riley pulled his starting quarterback. Harry Knight came off the bench to relieve Brock halfway through the third quarter and he threw two touchdown passes that beat the Lions, 22-20.

"I can tell you I wasn't very happy about it," said Brock about being benched. "When I became the starting quarterback, I never thought about being benched unless I was hurt or we were getting beaten badly. I always felt that as long as we were in the game, I could pull it out."

By mid-week, Riley hadn't decided who he was going to start their next game which was against Edmonton. He had said there was no disgrace in a player having a bad game and being replaced. He referenced the numerous times Ron Lancaster had his share of bad games, but the Riders didn't have anyone else to put in. The Blue Bombers did in Harry Knight and he was going to use him when needed.

"I knew my place," said Knight. "Brock and I were roommates the entire time I was with the Blue Bombers. We never really discussed who was better or who should play. We were both very competitive on the field and we both just wanted to win."

Brock shook off the mid-week controversy with an impressive performance in Edmonton. In the first half he was 8-10 and the offence had run the ball for 132 yards for a total of 249 yards. The Blue Bombers won 28-17 and seemed to be back on track.

Something had switched inside the quarterback. On the field, it was a new Ralph Brock. So new In fact, Ralph Brock no longer wanted to be called Ralph.

"We were questioning him like we always did after practice," said reporter Peter Young. "Someone asked him a question and he just looked down at the ground for a few moments. When he did look up at us, he asked, 'Do me a favour? Call me Dieter. That's my name.'"

"My full name is Ralph Dieter Brock," he said. "My father picked the name William when my older brother was born. When I came along, my mother figured it was her turn. But Dad wouldn't go for 'Dieter' so 'Ralph' was put first."

"I never really like Ralph," he said. "Everyone back home and my close friends always called me 'Diete.'

On the field, Dieter Brock started utilizing all the weapons he had at his disposal. He started taking what the defence was giving him and stayed away from the home run ball. Somewhere along the way, Brock realized that it wasn't all up to him. He didn't have to carry the weight of the world on his shoulders and he started spreading the work around.

In the next game, he took the renewed attitude and confidence and placed them on full display, embarrassing the Saskatchewan Roughriders, 28-10. The roles of the past had been reversed; Ron Lancaster was the one being totally frustrated, while Brock, who used to be impatient, suddenly realized that patience was a virtue, not to mention a formula for success if applied in the right situations.

In 1974, his hometown newspaper ran a small article announcing his Blue Bombers' signing, but it was overshadowed by the full page article proclaiming Muhammad Ali's win against Joe Frazier. Now, on the day when Muhammad Ali announced his retirement, Dieter Brock seemed to be coming of age.

But in the following game in Calgary, the Stampeders had obviously done their homework on the quarterback and shut him and the rest of the offence down, beating them 22-10. They knocked the offensive line aside and seemed to swallow up Brock on every down.

A few days later, a Winnipeg Free Press article by Don Blanchard targeting the Blue Bombers' offensive line, specifically, lineman Bill Frank, made its way around the locker room.

The article stated that Frank had mellowed in his old age and that the entire offensive line was old and decrepit and Lunsford was only keeping old has-beens like Frank around for sentimental reasons.

"Yeah, Bill read the article. We all did," said Brock. "The next day at the Bomber office, Bill confronted Blanchard. He said if Blanchard ever wrote about him again, he would, in not so many words, kill him. Blanchard was scared to death. He actually turned white when Bill was in his face."

"We always read the newspapers the next day after a game," said Brock. "We followed it all, newspaper, radio, TV. Some of it was upsetting and we'd get angry, but other times we thought it was quite funny."

"We used to listen to the Blue Bomber call-in show on CJOB with Bob Irving, Jack Matheson, Cactus Jack Wells and whoever else. They would discuss the last game and offer their opinions and suggestions on what was right or wrong with the guys. And people would call in and critique the game, coaches and the players."

"Myself, Butch Norman, Buddy Brown, Larry Butler and whoever else was around would be at my apartment listening and enjoying a few beers," Brock recalled. "It was hilarious because the guys would call in anonymously and discuss my play, good or bad."

On October 17, Brock called a perfect game against the Edmonton Eskimos, and the Blue Bombers won, 36-33, putting them in third place in the Western Conference. With a positive record of 7-6 for the season, Saskatchewan was up next.

Against the Roughriders, the young quarterback used a good balance of running and passing. He called a smart offensive game, while the Blue Bomber's defence frustrated the Roughriders' Lancaster again by holding his game back. The final score was 21-19, adding another win for the Blue Bombers.

The Montreal Alouettes were next on the schedule. The Blue Bombers led the game, 20-13 with five minutes left in the game. They had been on their own 32 yard line and the offence needed a big play or they would be forced to give the ball back to Montreal with good field position. On second and nineteen, Brock used his arm, connecting with Tom Scott for a 58 yard gain. On the next play, Bernie Ruoff kicked a field goal that put the game out of reach for the Alouettes with a score of 23-13.

Their next game against the B.C. Lions was a 23-17 win for the Blue Bombers leaving them with a record at 10-6 for the season and a spot in the playoffs. Brock would take a fist in the eye just after the beginning of the third quarter. "His eye was bleeding profusely so we took him out of the game and replaced him with Harry Knight," Coach Riley stated to the media after the game. "As far as we can ascertain, the fist didn't belong to one of our own Winnipeg players."

The Winnipeg Blue Bombers had earned a spot in the Western Conference playoffs, but they had to get through Edmonton first before taking on the Saskatchewan Roughrider again, which they had beaten all season.

There was no argument now; Ralph Brock had done more for his Winnipeg Blue Bombers in 1976 than Tom Wilkinson and Bruce Lemmerman combined, had done for their Eskimos. But going into what was being billed as the most important game of Brock's career; his maturity and experience were still being questioned.

And it was the Edmonton Eskimos who would answer those questions on the scoreboard with a narrow 14-12 win.

In the '76 Western Conference semi-final, the entire Blue Bombers' team just couldn't connect on the field. A perfect example was late in the fourth quarter when Brock threw and hit Bob LaRose at the Edmonton six yard line, but LaRose dropped the ball. Bernie Ruoff tried a field goal, but had to settle for a single point.

It also didn't help that Tom Wilkinson had his best game in three years, while Winnipeg's kicker hit one field goal in four attempts. The sudden death nail biter was won when Edmonton's Dave Cutler kicked a 53-yard field goal with less than three minutes left on the clock that made it 14-12 for the Eskimos.

The Eskimos had kept constant pressure on Brock and paid special attention to Tom Scott, his favoured target.

"It was a horrible loss," said Brock. "I played terrible and I really don't know why our passing game was so bad. I've watched that game several times since then and I looked awful. I was still a very inconsistent passer."

"But looking back at it now after having been a coach, the scheme in our passing game led to some throws that could really get you in trouble, especially for a young quarterback. We had played Edmonton pretty well earlier in the year and I think I had some good games against them, but not that time," said Brock. "And the worst thing was, if we had beaten them, we would have been playing Saskatchewan in the Western Final who we had beaten all three times that year."

"I left Winnipeg a few days after that game," he said. "But I carried that loss with me for a while."

Six weeks before the start of the Blue Bombers' 1977 training camp, Coach Riley announced that another quarterback would be in camp. Bill Bowerman from New Mexico State, who had been drafted by the Detroit Lions, but didn't make the team, would be in Winnipeg competing for a spot on the roster. Yes, Dieter Brock was the team's number one quarterback, but that didn't necessarily guarantee a starting job. It may have been implied, but that's not the same as earned.

This was the season in which Dieter Brock was going to have to prove that he measured up to some of the former great Winnipeg Blue Bomber quarterbacks like Rebholz, Sheley, Van Pelt, Ploen and Jacobs.

Adequate quarterbacking may provide a reasonable season for a football team, but it is great quarterbacking, the combination of intelligence, leadership and fundamentals that wins championships.

The 1977 Training Camp opened on June 2 with Harry Knight and Bill Bowerman while Brock competed in the CFL All-Star game in Toronto. He had been chosen to represent the Western Conference with Saskatchewan's Ron Lancaster.

Brock would show up on June 5 ready to play and lead his team. Head Coach Bud Riley welcomed him back, stating that having Brock in camp kept the receivers, especially the rookies more alert. "If they're not alert, Dieter is liable to stick a ball in their ear."

Offensive line coach Jim Erkenbeck had replaced Joe Faragalli in the off-season. The rookie coach from University of California at Berkley had coached Steve

Bartkowski who was with the Atlanta Falcons of the NFL. He had said that he doubted he would ever see another quarterback like Bartkowski who was known for his quick release and velocity, but he said he had now once he saw Brock.

On June 9, Bill Bowerman's knee went out and it was determined that he would not be able to return until the Blue Bombers were well into the season.

In an ironic twist of fate, rumours started coming out of Regina that the Roughriders had high hopes of luring former Auburn quarterback and Heisman trophy winner, Pat Sullivan to the team. But the San Francisco 49ers of the National Football League had purchased his contract from the Chicago Bears before the Roughriders could make a move. In late August of 1977, Sullivan was released from the 49ers, but he showed no interest in coming north to the CFL.

In the Blue Bombers' first pre-season game against Montreal, Knight took the reins and was spectacular in the 24-17 win. "I just wanted the opportunity to play," said Knight. "There was never any issues between Diete and I the whole time I was with Winnipeg."

The offensive line had been an area of concern to Riley and his assistants because of Bill Franks' retirement, but it seemed that things were working themselves out in training camp. The entire offence was impressive.

In the next pre-season game, a 27-19 victory against the Saskatchewan Roughriders, Knight started the first half and finished 5-11 with just 31 yards. Brock, in the second half finished 14-21 for 217 yards, proving he was number one and in command.

But this was football, where anything could happen at any time. In the B.C. game Brock went down on the first play of game. He was taken to hospital by ambulance, leaving the team with an unsettled feeling. But ten minutes after the team's 34-17 victory, Brock walked into the dressing room under his own steam.

"All I remember was being hit," he said. "I had numbing on my left side, which they diagnosed as a pinched nerve."

Cleared to play shortly after, it was no surprise that Brock would be the starting quarterback when the team faced the Roughriders in their first regular season game.

Brock completed 21 passes and ran for 26 yards in the impressive 33-11 win at Winnipeg Stadium. Six days later, in Edmonton, Brock passed for two second quarter touchdowns as the Blue Bombers would beat the Eskimos, 29-26.

On that same day, Brock's boyhood hero, Joe Namath was attending his first workout with the Los Angeles Rams in the NFL.

Nine days later, at the Winnipeg Stadium, in a rematch against the Eskimos, Brock was sacked five times. He seemed alone on field and Coach Riley sent Harry Knight in as relief in the third quarter. Despite his effort, Knight wouldn't fare any better. Brock was sent back in the fourth and managed to complete two touchdown passes to Tom Scott, but it was too little, too late. The Blue Bombers finished the game, 43-13 in their first loss of the season.

Against Montreal, Winnipeg fumbled the ball three times and gave up three interceptions losing 27-10. With two minutes left in the second quarter, Brock was pulled and replaced with Knight, again.

It was well known that Dieter Brock, an introverted individual, was inclined to take a loss hard and remain silent. Even when the team did win, he had less to say than any other player on the team. But losing his position and a game was a double disappointment. Giving Brock the hook and replacing him with Knight was one of the worst things Coach Riley could have done for Brock's confidence.

Riley had expected more consistency in Brock's third season. He complained that Brock didn't take advantage of his running ability and that his passes were often erratic.

In the next game, Harry Knight started and finished his first CFL game, but was beaten down by the B.C. Lions rush, losing 25-17.

Against the Calgary Stampeders the following week, Brock, who had lost his number one status the previous week, was as sharp as he'd ever been. He moved the ball one way or another for a total of 584 yards; the team's biggest output in years. They ran for 294 yards and Brock threw for 303 more. The highlight of the game came in the dying minutes of the third quarter with Brock lined up on his own 12 yards line. He hit Tom Scott at mid-filed on a 98-yard touchdown play, giving the Blue Bombers a 35-12 win.

On August 30, against the Hamilton Tiger-Cats, the Blue Bombers should have put the game away in the first half, but they didn't. The Blue Bombers had 290 yards of offence while the Tiger-Cats had just 86, but they had an interception, a fumble and a blocked punt. Brock had put together an almost flawless assault in the first thirty minutes of the game, but he stalled in the second half. Riley again tried Knight, but the back-up could only complete two of his five passes and had a sixth picked off by the Hamilton defence. Riley went back to Brock and an eventual tight 20-19 win.

On September 5, the Saskatchewan Roughriders beat the Blue Bombers 25-18. It was the first time in two seasons the Roughriders had beaten the Blue Bombers at Taylor Field. The game had been in doubt right until the final few minutes. The Blue Bombers needed eight points to win and they started their drive from the Roughriders' 46 yard line. Brock threw a 14 yard pass to Tom Scott, then a 12 yard to Jay Washington. On the last play of the game, he sent everyone deep, but Saskatchewan's Bill 'The Undertaker' Baker jumped a blocker and buried Brock into the turf before he could unload the ball.

Six days later, back at Winnipeg Stadium, the Blue Bombers took their revenge on the Roughriders, beating them in a 39-17 blow-out. Brock had completed just five of his eighteen passes, but three of them were for touchdowns.

Against Calgary, Brock managed to complete just six of twenty passes before giving Knight a chance with just over nine minutes left in the game. Knight, who went 6-11, had no success putting points on the board in a 16-10 loss, leaving the Blue Bombers with record of 5-5 for the season.

They would go on to beat Ottawa 36-24, and B.C. 19-15, before losing 31-24 to the Eskimos. A three game winning streak against Toronto, Calgary and B.C. would put them at 10-6 for the season.

In the B.C. win, Brock had one of his finest games of the season picking apart the Lions defence. With just five minutes left to play, the Blue Bombers tried to protect their 28-21 lead. They faced a third down with a yard and a half to go and to everyone's surprise, Riley made the decision not to punt and told Brock to go for it. He threw deep to Washington for the first down and six plays later, the Blue Bombers had a field goal, putting the game out of reach for the Lions. The final score was 31-21 for the Blue Bombers.

Brock had thrown 23-33 for 347 yards. His three touchdown passes against the Lions had raised his total to twenty-three for the season, making him the league's leader. Closest to him was Ottawa's Tom Clements with sixteen.

Brock had a completion average .578 which beat out Ron Lancaster. Tom Wilkinson had finished first, but he had thrown 264 passes compared to Brock's 418.

At the close of the 1977 regular season it was Edmonton. B.C. and Winnipeg, in that order, and the scene was set for the playoffs in the Western division. The three teams had all finished with 10-6 records, the first three way tie in the league since 1951. When mathematics entered into it using points for and against in the games involving the three teams, the Winnipeg Blue Bombers would finish third and would have to face the B.C. Lions again.

Unfortunately, the Blue Bombers had history against them going into the game. Since the Western conference had expanded to five teams in 1954, the team that finished third had only won the championship twice. Two out of twenty-three were pretty tough odds.

By the end of game, the odds were correct. The B.C. Lions beat the Blue Bombers, 33-32 to end their 1977 season. The Lions defence got to Brock every time they could and the Blue Bombers' running game was also shut down.

There was one play in particular in the playoff game that still haunts Brock to this day. With 1:33 left to play, the B.C. Lions Joe Fourqurean reached into the air to

knock away a third-down pass intended for the Blue
Bombers' receiver, Mike Holmes.

"I still think about that play," said Brock. "If
Fourqurean's reach had of been just a few inches shorter,
we would have taken that game because there was nothing
between Holmes and the end zone."

Three days later, while most were still coming to terms
with the heartbreaking loss, the Winnipeg Football Club
made a shocking decision. The official team statement
read, 'The Management committee of the football club met
today and decided unanimously not to renew Bud Riley's
contract. Bud had given us an entertaining team in the last
three or four seasons, but we felt the 1977 team could
possibly have gone further than it did.'

"That was tough," said Brock. "Just when we seemed to
have things going our way, that happened. I was surprised
and concerned at the same time. He was a good coach."

"When Bud was fired, the reason I was upset more than
anything was that I thought we had a really good team," he
said. "Jay Washington was one of the leading rushers in
the league and Tommy Scott and Gordy Patterson were one
and two in the league in receptions. Tommy had caught ten
touchdown passes for over a thousand yards so we had a
very good offence. We had more wins than any team in the
league over the last two years so I didn't understand the
firing. Now we were going to be starting all over again with
a new coach and changes. Yeah, I was pissed off and so
we're a lot of other players."

Chapter Nine

Just a few hours after the Blue Bombers' Bud Riley announcement, replacement names started running through the rumour mill. Names of Ron Lancaster, Eagle Keys, Ray Jauch, Cal Murphy and surprisingly, even Don Jonas were being thrown around.

By late November, General Manager Earl Lunsford stated that he had set a mid-January deadline for acquiring a new head coach for the team and had received permission from several other teams to start personnel discussions.

On December 1, Edmonton's Ray Jauch quietly slid into Winnipeg to meet with Lunsford to discuss the coaching position and by December 5 their discussions were over. The Winnipeg Blue Bombers' had secured the thirty-nine year old Jauch as the new Winnipeg Blue Bombers' Head Coach.

His credentials were impressive; so impressive, in fact, that the team gave him a three year contract. It was the longest coaching contract ever offered by the Winnipeg club since the Bud Grant era.

As a former Winnipeg Blue Bomber player, Ray Jauch's career had been cut short when he tore his Achilles tendon in the 1961 Grey Cup game. That began his career in coaching, first with the Winnipeg Rods in 1962, before moving to the University of Iowa two years later.

Ray Jauch became an assistant coach in Edmonton in 1968 and two years later accepted the position of head coach. During his seven years in Edmonton, Jauch had guided the Eskimos to the Western Conference play-offs six times and to the Grey Cup three times. He was named coach of the year by the CFL in 1970. The Eskimos finally won the Grey Cup on their third attempt at the big game in 1975.

Jauch had decided to end his coaching term at the end of the 1978 season with an over-all record of 63-43-4, to accept the position of manager of football operations.

During the Winnipeg press conference announcing his new role, Jauch stated, "I had achieved the things I set out to do from the sidelines and wanted an opportunity to view things from a managerial standpoint. I didn't, however, foresee just how much I would miss coaching. But I am sure that what I have learned during the past year will be a great help in my new position here. I have always liked a challenge and there is certainly one here."

While Jauch's appointment made the club's management team happy, there were concerns in the player ranks. It's no secret that veteran players do not like coaching changes. They can introduce an element of uncertainty and insecurity into the locker room. Head coaches usually make their inaugural season decisions based on a player's performance history from the previous year, while new coaches make them on what they see in training camp. They do not want "leftover" egos and spats from a previous team to interfere with their plans. That meant Blue Bomber veterans would have to work harder in camp under a new coach, rather than rely on their previous history. With a new coach, nothing is guaranteed, no matter how an individual has performed in the past.

"I feel the team has some excellent personnel," Jauch was quoted as saying. "But it appears the big problem was getting over the hump, winning the big game. That's the hurdle I will have to get the team over."

His philosophy to address those concerns was to utilize all aspects of the team's final 33-man roster after training camp. Jauch had said he was prepared to give all his players a chance to contribute and that philosophy was going to be applied to his quarterbacks as well. He repeatedly said that he wouldn't hesitate at any time to try the two quarterback system he had successfully established in Edmonton with Tom Wilkinson and Bruce Lemmerman.

"I believe a two-quarterback system is a great advantage if used properly," said Jauch when asked about the Blue Bombers' system. "From the standpoint that Ralph Brock was number one last season, I would hope he comes into training camp with that in mind. But I have never hesitated to switch quarterbacks if one was having difficulty getting the ball into the end zone. That's what it is all about. I see no reason why both Winnipeg quarterbacks cannot contribute to winning."

It was no surprise that both Blue Bomber quarterbacks, Brock and Knight, were not big fans of Jauch's idea. Brock had stated his position from the beginning, but Knight had been a little more reserved with his opinion.

"As far as the two-quarterback system, I didn't like it" said Brock. "I knew that is what he had been doing in Edmonton and when he was hired to replace Bud, I wasn't thrilled. I went to Earl Lunsford and expressed my dissatisfaction and told him that I wasn't going to play in a two-quarterback system. I also remember telling Ray the same thing. I actually went in and told Coach Jauch and Earl that I wanted to be traded if that's what they were going to do."

"I led the CFL in touchdown passes with twenty-three and had the second highest completion percentage at 58 percent in the 1977 season. Jerry Tagge from the Lions had been named the All CFL quarterback, but I had nine more touchdown passes and threw for more yards and more completions. Plus I had a higher completion percentage."

"I felt like if I was the best quarterback, then I should be in the game as long as we had a chance to win it. If they felt like somebody else was better than me, then that guy should be the starting quarterback and play the game."

"The two-quarterback system would probably work if you had two quarterbacks that were agreeable to doing that," said Brock. "And they probably would agree to that because neither one of them was better than the other. But in my mind I was the best quarterback and I wanted to play."

"Ray came to my home in Birmingham so we could talk. He asked me to just give things a chance," said Brock.

"To be honest, I reluctantly went back that season because I had nowhere else I could go. I really felt like I was the best quarterback in the league after having back to back seasons of 10 wins and 5 losses and finishing second in the league in passing behind Ronnie Lancaster in 1976."

Brock wasn't the only one unhappy. Harry Knight had indicated at the end of the 1977 season that he would rather play out his option than sign for another year with the Blue Bombers as a non-playing backup. Earl Lunsford had indicated that he wasn't anticipating any difficulty in re-signing Knight, but his future would probably be determined by Jauch's talks with the backup.

"Coach Jauch did come to Virginia to see me," said Knight. "He asked me to come back and at least give it chance."

At 24 years-old, Harry Knight had already proven himself and was being labeled by some around the league as the brightest young quarterback in the CFL.

He had lived in the shadow of Brock since he had arrived in Winnipeg, but there was little animosity from the guy who had been number two and trying.

"It was something I just accepted. I knew what I was getting into the first day I showed up in Winnipeg," said Knight. "I wanted to play and I wanted to win. I had been cut by the Oakland Raiders right in the airport waiting to head to Dallas to play. That was such a disappointment and I didn't want to go through that again."

"I remember on my first day in Winnipeg, sitting between Dieter and Ealey in the locker room. I knew then it was going to be difficult, but I had to accept that if I ever wanted the opportunity to play, even though I didn't agree with it all the time."

"Of course there were times when I thought I should have been put in games sooner," he said. "It's not an easy job going in with two or three minutes left in a game and trying to pull out a win. But after my discussion with Ray, I agreed to come back."

By February, Jauch had come to terms with both Knight and Brock, both quarterbacks had agreed to multiyear contracts. "Both of them were so focused on winning and that made my job easier," said Jauch.

With his quarterbacks secured, the new head coach moved forward in an attempt to putting his own stamp on the team, but it wasn't an easy task. All Star receiver and Brock's favourite target, Tom Scott had made it known that he wasn't happy in Winnipeg. He was finally dealt to Edmonton for a relatively unknown prospect at the time by the name of Joe Poplawski.

In another surprising twist, veteran centre, Bob Swift walked into Lunsford's office and announced his retirement. Swift had played seven years with the Blue Bomber and was a three-time CFL All-Star and four-time West Division All-Star.

With Swift's retirement, John Bonk was moved from his defensive position to the offensive line to fill that hole. Hometown rookie, Leo Ezerins was given the opportunity to grab a spot on defence.

Going into training camp, Jauch made no secret of the fact that he had three areas of concern that he was going to address. He felt the Blue Bombers were far too susceptible to the big play, they had inconsistent field goal kicking; and they lacked pass protection.

Their first pre-season game was a 23-14 win against the Saskatchewan Roughriders, but the second was a 34-4 loss against the Argonauts.

After the two pre-season games, Jauch could tell that his concerns still had not been addressed. He described his team as sloppy and he saw even more problems. Brock was having trouble finding receivers and getting the ball to them. He was throwing high, low and out of bounds. Jauch had said he was going spend time watching to see if the receivers were running the correct routes and if Brock was reading the defence correctly.

The pieces seemed to come together in their 21-10 victory over the Calgary Stampeders and after the fourth and last pre-season game, it seemed like Jauch finally had his house in order. Against Ottawa, Brock seemed to regain his accuracy and the offensive line gave both Brock and Knight ample time to read the defence and complete their passes. It was a close 28-27 win for the Blue Bombers, but it was a win both on the field and in the locker room.

"Everyone seemed to be settling in," said John Bonk. "And Dieter was taking control in the huddle. He never did have to say much. His confidence spoke it all. Besides, with that accent, we couldn't understand what he was saying anyway."

But that was the pre-season when nothing really mattered. In their first regular season game against B.C., the Lion's defensive back, Drew Taylor broke through the line and sacked Brock and Knight four times. The rest of the B.C. pack was able to get to them six times in total.

Brock had started the game, but completed just three of his six passes. True to his philosophy, Coach Jauch wasted no time pulling him out and replacing him with Knight, who finished the game. Jauch had said that Brock was simply not moving the ball. Knight had a reasonable amount of success, but the team still lost, 30-14.

After the game, a disheartened Brock stated that he was a slow starter and felt he wasn't given enough time to establish himself.

In their second game, Jauch chose to start Knight against the coach's former team, the Edmonton Eskimos, but he wasn't able to establish an offensive attack during the first half. The Blue Bombers managed just three first downs and 39 yards of total offence. Brock replaced Knight late in the second quarter and managed to move the ball, but his efforts would still not be enough. The Blue Bombers did manage to bounce back before finally succumbing 29-28 to the Eskimos. It was their second straight loss, while the Eskimos were now 2-0. After the game, Edmonton head coach, Hugh Campbell, raved about his new quarterback, Warren Moon.

In practice the following week, Harry Knight injured his shoulder and was forced off the practice field. The diagnosis was a torn rotator cuff that would sideline him for several games. Local University of Manitoba quarterback, Bud Harden was called in as insurance in case Knight was unable to play in the next game. Jauch had seen Harden early in training camp, but he had been released early.

In the team's next game, two explosive plays; a 70 yard and a 90 yard pass from Brock to Richard Crump, and three field goals from Bernie Ruoff gave the Blue Bombers their first victory of the season, a 23-13 win against the Saskatchewan Roughriders. It was noted that Brock was now getting his best protection in the season so far.

And that protection carried over against Hamilton when the Blue Bombers gained another 29-7 win.

Knight's shoulder was not responding to treatment as much as Jauch had hoped, so he brought in Ken Smith, an import quarterback, on a five day trial. Smith had been a twelfth round pick of the Denver Broncos and was a recent cut from the team.

After four games, rookie Blue Bombers' receiver, Joe Poplawski was the league's leading receiver with 286 yards on ten catches. Brock seemed to have found his new favourite target.

A 29-21 loss to Calgary was not what the team had expected next, especially when they knew Edmonton was their next battle. In that game, the Blue Bombers were down by six, with plenty of time left on the clock. From inside their own midfield mark, Brock threw deep to Holmes. He got his hands on the ball, but he was never in control. After a quick juggle, he dropped it and the Blue Bombers lost to the Eskimos, 14-8.

Despite an ankle injury in the last minute of the game, Brock had competed 64 per cent of his passes for 300 yards. "Brock played a helluva game," Jauch was quoted as saying after the loss. "I get more respect for that guy every time we play. He played against the best defence in the league and under terrible conditions and what a job he did."

Harry Knight's shoulder was still not allowing the quarterback to throw with the intensity the offence needed. Ken Smith had not worked out, so the team brought in Dee Jay Donlin, a recent Minnesota Vikings' cut, to back up Brock.

The Blue Bombers offence would go on to score four times against the Alouettes on passes by Brock and beat the former Grey Cup Champions 36-10.

On September 4, in Regina, the Blue Bombers clung to a tight 24-22 lead late in the fourth quarter. Stuck at their own seven yard line, Brock sent running back Richard Crump off-tackle with the ball. Crump went 103 yards downfield for the touchdown, giving the Blue Bombers another victory and putting their record at 5-4. The pieces to Jauch's puzzle were finally coming together.

By mid-September, three Blue Bomber players led the league in their respective categories; Brock for passing, Poplawski in receiving yards and Richard Crump in rushing. Poplawski, the youngest receiver in the league was also the hottest, having caught 49 passes in ten games. Brock had 2,335 in yardage with twelve touchdown passes. He had also thrown the longest touchdown pass at 90 yards. Vince Phason and Crump also led the league in kick-off returns

The longest run from scrimmage in the league was the 103 yard touchdown run by Crump in their last game against Saskatchewan. The team had thrown more passes, 335, and completed 200, more than any other team in the league. Net passing yardage was well ahead of everyone else at 2,562.

With the Toronto Argonauts coming to town, the Winnipeg team was certainly on a high. They were on a two game winning streak and knew there were could be more victories to come.

Back-up quarterback, Dee Jay Donlin had not panned out and was replaced by Terry Luck. Luck, with impressive credentials from Nebraska and the NFL's Cleveland Browns, had joined the team after the final cuts from Cleveland. Injured in the '76 season, he had moved to coaching at North Texas and Washington State. He had shown Jauch enough in his three day trial that the coach felt comfortable releasing Donlin.

But a back-up wasn't needed as Brock led the Blue Bombers to their third straight victory in a 19-14 win against the Argonauts.

"Knowing that I was going to be in there the whole game meant now that I could relax and just play the game," said Brock. "I didn't have to try to make something big happen every time. I think it also showed Coach Jauch that he could depend on just one quarterback and not have to use a two quarterback system all the time."

"Certainly playing in Coach Jauch's system was tailor-made for my throwing ability. But one of the key things to being an outstanding quarterback is accuracy throwing the football and not necessarily having a great arm. The more that you can use the whole field with your arm, the better you will be. Bud Riley's offence was more of a half field throwing offence. It was great for handling blitzes, but I think it was prone to cause more interceptions because the field was kind of cut in half. With Ray Jauch, his system allowed me to use the whole field, which gave me more space and really cut my interceptions down."

"I really believe Ray and I were very similar. We were both stubborn," said Brock. "Even though our relationship didn't start out well, I think we both began to understand each other. We both wanted to win. And as he got to know me, he knew how much playing the game meant to me. He realized that I was a team player, even though I wanted to be the starting and only quarterback. But Ray was the one who started putting the pieces together that would make me a much better quarterback and give us a much better offence and a better chance to win it all."

"He got to know how tough I was and how hard I took losing and not playing. Toughness is another one of the key traits of great quarterbacks. You have to be able to keep your eyes focused down-field and not worry about the pass rush so you can deliver the ball just as you're about to get hit."

"When you understand your offensive your system you should be able to go to the area where you have the best chance of completing passes. The more you understand your offence, the better you will be as a quarterback. And you can only gain that knowledge through practice and playing the game. But playing the game is the most crucial piece to gaining that knowledge. The more you play and the longer you play, the better you get."

"After some experience, you understand what the defence is going to do, but that comes after you have played in the system for a few years. You have to have the talent to get that opportunity. And once you get the opportunity you don't have long to get it right."

His understanding of Jauch's system allowed Brock to throw four touchdown passes to lead the Winnipeg attack against the B.C. Lions the next game. Mike Holmes and Joe Poplawski split the touchdown honours receiving two each. Brock completed 15-19 for 276 yards. This time when Lions' Joe Fourqurean's hand got in the way, the ball bounced right into the arms of Joe Poplawski, giving the Blue Bombers the 32-25 win.

Six days later the Blue Bombers faced the Lions again in Vancouver. Inside Empire Stadium, Brock completed nine passes for 101 yards and three touchdowns and the Lions never had a chance to recover. The final score was 38-27 for the Blue Bombers.

After the game, Jauch was quoted as saying "B.C. quarterback, Tagge threw rainbows while, Brock, who puts something on the ball, can complete a lot of passes."

"The fire in that boy's eyes was something I will never forget," said Jauch. "I'd never seen anything like that before and don't think I ever will. He was extremely quiet and sometimes it was difficult to get anything out of him, but his intensity certainly made up for that. And he had the ability to carry that intensity into the huddle without saying too much at all."

"When he had that look, you didn't question him," said center, John Bonk. "When Dieter called the play, you did it. No discussion."

After the B.C. win, the Blue Bombers went on a six game winning streak and prepared to go against Edmonton once again.

The Eskimos' head coach, Hugh Campbell was quoted as saying before the game, "Only a fool would ignore all the weapons they have at their disposal. They have so many ways of moving the ball. On top of all those excellent receivers and two quality running backs they have the best quarterback in the Canadian Football League in Ralph Brock. Their receivers need to get open by only one step and Brock will hit them right in the chest. He's got such a powerful arm, the only way to stop him is to get to him before he has a chance to unload."

"Dieter was the only quarterback I know who could make the ball whistle as it went through the air," recalls Jauch.

Prior to the game, Edmonton veteran quarterback Tom Wilkinson and rookie Warren Moon had combined to complete 234 of 414 passes for 3039, a 56.5 per cent completion average. Brock had completed 221 of 357 passes for 2811 yards for a 61.9 per cent completion average.

Both teams struggled early in the game and at the end of the first quarter, the score was tied, 4-4. The Blue Bombers lead briefly 7-4 in the second, but Wilkinson hit former Blue Bomber Tom Scott for a touchdown that put the Eskimos back in the lead. The Blue Bombers failed to score again until the final play of the third quarter, but by then the Eskimos' twenty had put the game out of reach. The Blue Bombers lost, 38-10.

Next, against Saskatchewan, the Blue Bombers lost possession twice on downs and Brock threw four interceptions early in the game. But Winnipeg came back in the fourth quarter on two field goals and a two yard touchdown run by Brock. After the game, he was the first to admit it wasn't one of his best performances. He completed 20 of 35 passes, but threw four interceptions in their 13-7 win.

At that point in his career, what impressed people the most was Brock's growth in maturity. He had made great strides that season. Asked what went wrong in certain situations, he would never transfer the blame to others and always took the majority of it himself. When he didn't play well, he said so.

By the time Calgary came to town for the next game, both teams were vying for second place spot in the Western Conference. The game was close and the Blue Bombers came within four points of winning the spot. Brock completed 21 of 33 for 262 yards. He connected with Holmes for two touchdowns of 38 and 24 yards and Patterson from 5 yards out. But it was Calgary's running game that outperformed the Blue Bombers that day.

Despite the loss, Jauch once again praised the work of his quarterback. "He has the innate ability to connect deep and we have various deep patterns in our plans. I wouldn't want to take that away from him. I thought he played very well. I'm not disappointed in him at all. If the long bombs are successful you look great. When they don't, they aren't worth anything."

In the final regular season game, the Blue Bombers would have to face Calgary again. This was their opportunity to set the record straight after the last loss and prove who deserved second place.

But on the eighth play of the fourth quarter, in what was a tight game, Brock would go down.

"I did a three-step drop, planted my right foot and stepped out with my left," he recalls. "Just as my left foot hit the turf and I was about to release the ball, John Helton had snuck through the line and hit my left knee."

Minutes later, in a silent Winnipeg Stadium, Dieter Brock was carried off the field by two teammates. The immediate diagnosis was stretched knee ligaments. "I knew right away, as soon as I was hit," he said. "It wasn't good."

With Harry Knight still injured, rookie Terry Luck was called in to take over. But he was swallowed up by the Calgary defence and suffered a severely bruised shoulder. He was unable to throw the ball for the rest of game and the Blue Bombers would go down, 22-14. But the good news was they had secured a spot in the play-offs. The bad news was it was against Calgary and they didn't have an experienced quarterback.

Dr. Wayne Hildahl, the Blue Bombers' doctor, confirmed that Brock would not be available for the play-off game. In fact, he said Brock would not be able to play again in 1978. It would be the first time Dieter Brock would miss a game because of an injury since his playing days in high school.

Coach Jauch had no choice but to start Harry Knight with Luck as the back-up. Knight hadn't thrown in a game since he went down July 18 and when it was all over, the Blue Bombers would lose the game, 38-4. Without their starting quarterback they were rendered almost completely helpless by Calgary's hard-hitting and emotionally inspired defence lead by John Helton and Reggie Lewis.

The Calgary defence hammered the Blue Bombers offence into dropping the ball six times and they recovered three of them.

"I was in a cast from my upper thigh to my foot," said Brock. "I couldn't fly so that meant I had to watch the game from home. It was a horrible way to end the season."

But when the season was over and the numbers compiled, they showed that Dieter Brock had been the busiest passer in the CFL for the second consecutive year. He had edged out Edmonton's Tom Wilkinson by a single point over the six categories which determine the passing ratings. Brock finished first in two categories completing 294 passes, the third highest one-season total ever in the CFL behind Peter Liske's record of 303 in 1976 and Ron Lancaster's 297 in 1976. Brock also led the league in total yardage at 3,755. He finished the season with a 60% completion record, 18 interceptions and 23 touchdown passes.

On December 18, the cast was removed. "At first, I couldn't even bend my knee," he said. "I knew I had some work ahead of me in the off-season in Birmingham. I didn't have a recuperative program set-up and I preferred to play it by ear. I mostly did running on the spot and skipping rope, adding squat exercises later around mid-February."

While Brock was recuperating in Birmingham, back in Winnipeg, a block-buster trade had taken place with the Calgary Stampeders. The Blue Bombers gave up Richard Crump, Lyall Woznesensky and Mervin Walker for John Helton and John Malinosky.It was undoubtedly the biggest trade and most significant transaction the Canadian

Football League had seen since the Blue Bombers and Hamilton Tiger-Cats swapped Don Jonas for Chuck Ealey.

The irony of the whole situation was that John Helton was the one responsible for putting Brock out of action and forcing the Blue Bombers into the play-offs without their quarterback.

Chapter Ten

"I never blamed John Helton for my injury. I never thought of him as a dirty player. Not at all," said Brock, recalling the off-season trade. "Richard had been an outstanding, all around running back, but I thought getting a Hall of Fame defensive lineman had to be a tremendous benefit to our defence and our team."

"That hit was just of those things that sometimes couldn't be avoided," he continued. "It was one of those plays that happen so quick it was hard to make any adjustments. So, no, I didn't have any hard feeling to Helton. Hell, I was glad we got him so we wouldn't have to play against him anymore. Here is one of the best d-linemen in the league, and now, he's on our team."

Helton, Brock and 79 other players in camp were signed and expected to report to the 1979 Winnipeg Blue Bombers' Training Camp. Coach Jauch made it known to all that there were openings going into camp in almost every aspect of the team, except for a handful of players.

Even before camp had started, Brock was the obvious number one quarterback with Harry Knight and Terry Luck expected to battle it out for the back-up position. But Luck failed his physical because of a shoulder injury the day before camp opened.

Moorhead State's Ed Shultz was a bright prospect in camp that was expected to make an impact. Shultz had spent time in 1978 training camp with Oakland and scrimmaged against Dallas and the L.A. Rams.

On June 7, Winnipeg acquired quarterback Ken Washington from the Saskatchewan Roughriders for future considerations.

Washington was a graduate of North Texas State and was one of five quarterbacks in the Roughriders camp. He had tried out with the Saskatchewan team the previous year but was cut.

Knight's shoulder was still giving him problems and the pressure of the year old injury had taken its toll on the 25 year-old quarterback and he grew more frustrated each day. "I don't want to give up, but I can't keep up this way," he was quoted as saying.

Brock experienced some pain in his knee early in the first few days of camp, but it didn't seem to bother his performance. Because of that, Coach Jauch chose to start Brock in the first pre-season against the Calgary Stampeders. Ed Shultz had his turn with the offence, but when he couldn't move the ball, Brock was sent back in the third quarter. The Blue Bombers would drop their first outing, 35-13.

The team would run through two more pre-season losses against, Ottawa, 13-12 and B.C., 12-6 before winning their last outing against Saskatchewan, 16-10.

Bill Troup, who had been dropped by the Baltimore Colts of the NFL, was brought into camp near the end of June. Five years earlier, Troup had been in the Calgary Stampeders' training camp, but was released when Peter Liske returned to the team. He had first caught on with the Philadelphia Eagles and then the Baltimore Colts.

After the pre-season, there was no doubt that Brock would be number one. Unfortunately, Harry Knight's shoulder issues continued throughout the pre-season and he was forced to announce his retirement.

"I loved playing in Winnipeg," Knight said. "I have no regrets at all. My wife is from there so how could I?"

Ed Schultz had not made an impression with the coaching staff and was released, leaving Bill Troup in the back-up position.

The Blue Bombers first regular season game was against Edmonton and the Eskimos immediately showed that their defence had not lost a step from the previous year. The Blue Bombers' running game was almost non-existent for the most part and Brock was harassed every time he stepped back with the ball. The Eskimos defence sacked him four times and he finished 19-34 for 191 yards. Tom Wilkinson finished 21-31 for 335 yards leaving the final score in favour of the Eskimos, 28-10.

The second game was almost a continuation of the first except this time it was the Stampeders. Their defence broke through and sacked Brock seven times. By the end of the first quarter Calgary had built up a 15-3 lead and were ahead 23-6 in the second half. The Blue Bombers managed just 104 yards of net offence including 26 on the ground. Brock left the game with a first degree knee sprain in his left knee. Joe Poplawski, the team's leading receiver left with two broken bones in his ankle and would be out for ten weeks.

The Blue Bombers were now winless in their first two regular season games. Coach Jauch was quoted in the media saying, "The only way to go is up," said Jauch.

With Brock on the sidelines, Bill Troup started against the B.C. Lions. He threw two touchdown passes and wasn't sacked at all. He finished the game 15-22. He took charge behind a tougher, protective shield and called a good game, but the Blue Bombers still lost, 19-18.

Troup started in the next game against Montreal, but with two and half minutes left in the second quarter, he was pulled and replaced with Brock. He was effective with short five and six yard gains, but he grew impatient and attempted a few long ones. The Blue Bombers would go down again, 25-10.

After the game, a solemn Brock spoke to media. "We've always moved the ball," he said. "Teams feared our offence. It used to be nothing for us to score 30 points. But for the life of me, I can't understand what's going on

The day before the next game, during the coach's press conference, Jauch stated, "I have no reservations regarding our quarterbacks. We might just start Brock and let him do what he can. If he has trouble, we'll let him stand on the sidelines and take a look at it all with Billy Troup at quarterback. Right now there is no set plan and I won't hesitate to make changes."

Brock did start against the Ticats. He was shaky during the first couple of sequences, but once he settled in and took control, the Hamilton defenders were helpless. He was confident and patient directing the Winnipeg offence to the team's first win.

"It felt like we were back to the old times," said Brock after the win. "I may have lost a step at the beginning but I never lost my confidence."

One of the hardest adjustments an American quarterback must make is to develop the patience that's required to move the ball in a three down system. Most American born quarterbacks have had the four down game instilled in them at a young age and it becomes hard for them to move the ball with one less opportunity. Panic sets in and mistakes can be made.

Against Edmonton, the Eskimos jumped ahead by eight points and, as Jauch later stated, some of the Winnipeg players seemed to quit. Jauch was incensed and irate on the sideline as he watched his football team go into the second half of the game and give the Eskimos an easy victory.

Blue Bombers' slotback, Gord Paterson became the target of Jauch's anger and was banished to the locker room during the third quarter.

"I don't know exactly what was going on between Gordy and Coach Jauch," Brock said. "But it probably stemmed from all the changes that were being made. A lot of us saw where Ray had gotten rid of a lot of Bud Riley's players and I think Gord was more vocal about it or maybe he just gave off a certain attitude towards Ray. Ray could feel it was affecting the team."

"Paterson was being disciplined, that's all," Jauch told the media following the game. "He doesn't quite understand who is running this football team. I do not care to comment any more. It's a personal thing between Gord and me."

The 'personal thing' most likely had stemmed from a sideline comment that Jauch was in no mood to hear while his team fell apart on the field.

"One quitter is too many," Jauch had said. "And whether it's one, two, three or whatever, it will be corrected. This team has got to learn how to fight back."

A few days later, Gord Paterson was sent to Hamilton. In his six years with the Blue Bombers, Paterson had been one of the top Canadian performers for the team. He caught 69 passes in the previous season alone.

"I've said before that was a very difficult year," said Brock. "When you bring a new coach in, he's going to get players that he feels fits his team and that's just the way it is."

Things quickly changed a few days later against the Roughriders. Winnipeg scored on their first possession on a Dieter Brock pass to Walt Passaglia. Brock then threw touchdown passes of 47 yards and 13 yards to Mike Holmes, guiding the team to beat Saskatchewan, 30-1.

Seven days later, in a rematch against the same Riders, the Blue Bombers took advantage of the Saskatchewan's weak defence and built an early lead. At one point the Blue Bombers' offence was second and 14 at their own 42 yard line when Brock hit Passaglia with a 47 yard bomb to the Saskatchewan 21. Six plays later, Brock dove in for the touchdown and a 21-10 lead. The Roughriders never came back, losing 28-11.

The following week, at Winnipeg Stadium, 27,203 Blue Bomber fans witnessed their quarterback limp off the field in the third quarter of the game. Brock had just thrown a six-yard touchdown pass to Mike Holmes when B.C. Lions defensive back, Drew Taylor tackled him in the backfield. Early indications were that the injury was not serious, but it was the same knee that had given him problems all season. Bill Troup was sent in, but he was unable make a difference and Bombers lost 17-15.

Brock was able to start against the Ottawa Rough Riders the next week. The Rough Riders trailed from the opening kick-off, but managed to score 11 points in the last 1:03 and defeat the Blue Bombers 22-19.

Brock missed the last 4:33 of the game when his knee gave out again, after taking a sack from Larry Brune and a few other Rough Riders who piled on. Billy Troup went in for last two series, but couldn't keep the ball for a sustained drive. The Blue Bombers now had a record of 3-7 for the season.

Following the game, Coach Jauch came to his quarterback's rescue with the media. "I know the 'in' thing now will be to knock Brock because that's the way it is around here. I thought Brock had a helluva game in the first half with all that pressure we let them put on him," said Jauch. "Brock's a great human being and nobody on this team tries harder than he does, but I know they'll be on him tomorrow."

"There'll be some of you who don't understand, who'll knock Brock because that'll make you popular with the masses and I can't do anything about that. I just ask you to search yourselves and tell the truth. We didn't give Brock any help, and there's a lot more to an offence like that than just the quarterback."

A trend was starting throughout the city of Winnipeg spurred on by an editorial written by the Winnipeg Tribune's Jack Matheson. "Brock's A Crock" jeers could be heard from the stands and signs could be seen around the Winnipeg Stadium.

On September 19, it was confirmed that the Winnipeg Blue Bombers were shopping for a quarterback. They received a gloomy medical report on the condition of Brock's damaged left knee and felt they needed to do something. "We're not optimistic," said general manager Earl Lunsford at the press conference. "It's the same injury he's had before, but more severe. The knee is still tender and there may be some cartilage damage."

Against Calgary, Troup was the starter, but the best he could do was drive the offence close enough for a 22-yard field goal. Jauch turned to Brock who showed the masses exactly why he was number one. With a damaged knee, he led drives of 75, 72, and 69 yards. He also converted seven long second downs.

Late in the game, the Blue Bombers had three attempts at a first and three, but the Stampeders defence stopped them every time. On the last play of the game, they again had a first and three. Brock flipped the ball to Gervais, but he was immediately stripped of the ball. The final score was 18-13 in favour of Calgary, but Brock was impressive in his return.

They would lose again to the Lions 22-21 and in a Calgary rematch, 18-13.

In a 19-15 loss against Toronto, Brock threw three interceptions, Ricky Wesson fumbled a punt return and Bernie Ruoff missed a field goal with time running out. There were other mistakes like dropped passes from Passaglia and Holmes.

The season was already a washout when the Blue Bombers defeated the Saskatchewan Roughriders 23-14. They would close out the dismal season with a 19-11 loss to Edmonton

On Monday Oct 29, the 1979 Winnipeg Blue Bombers assembled for the final time at their annual wind up party. The fact that the date was before the start of the Western Conference play-offs certainly put a damper on the festivities.

For several, it would be their farewell and the last time they would be together. The team's 4-12 record almost guaranteed there would be new faces when the 1980 training camp opened.

"1979 was such a terrible year," he said. "Joe Pop got hurt and he was out. We had so many changes on the team and I was not a hundred percent and missed several games. I remember several players during the 1979 season when we got together that night talking about who would be there the next year. Nobody felt secure about coming back in 1980."

Brock was ready to get back to Birmingham and put the season behind him. He planned to undergo an intensive physical conditioning plan to strengthen his knee and an ailing shoulder.

"I've said before that I never lost confidence in my ability or my desire to win. That's something I couldn't afford to do regardless of what was going on around me. Confidence has to be part of your game whether it be in your arm or your ability to scramble and move around. It's something that allows you to stand out and says that 'you're the guy' to everyone else."

"You can have all the talent in the world, but if you don't have confidence in yourself and the desire to want to be the best, you're not going to make it."

Chapter Eleven

"That Jack Matheson article is total bullshit!"

In late November of 1979, several members of the Winnipeg media somehow managed to get wind of a letter that Brock had supposedly written to Coach Jauch when he returned home to Birmingham, demanding a trade. No one outside of Ray Jauch's office had actually seen the letter, but a few journalists decided to use their "editorial privilege" to speculate on its contents.

On November 28, 1979, Jack Matheson of the Winnipeg Tribune used his column to publically share his thoughts on the contents of the letter.

"The gist of the message, I am advised, is that Brock doesn't love the Blue Bombers, or Winnipeg, anymore and would like a change of scenery."

"It doesn't take a genius to suspect that Brock wasn't happy here last season, or that the 'Brock's a Crock' group finally got to him. Another quarterback with a more extroverted personality would tell the knockers to go to hell and he'd go out there and proceed to massage their tonsils with the football, but that isn't Brock's style."

"Brock is a very withdrawn, shy, sensitive young man and he broods a lot. If you're questioning whether a quarterback made this way can ever take command of a team and lead it to victory over the haul, so am I."

"That was all bull crap," said Brock, still irritated when he recalls the situation today. "First off, it's not that I didn't like Winnipeg or the Blue Bombers. That was far from the truth. I didn't like the situation the way it was going. I felt like we were going backwards after we had had one of the winningest teams in the league over the two-year period before Bud Riley was fired."

"Obviously, I didn't like the idea of a two-quarterback system," he said. "I had stated that from the beginning. But in 1978, it was averted because of Harry Knight's injury. In 1979, I never really got over my own injury from the year before and my knee gave me problems the entire season. We were losing and it was very discouraging and frustrating for all of us."

"No one was happy in the 1979 season," he said. "How could you be when you've finished the season with a 4-12 record, you've got injuries and players are getting released? I thought about saying something at the end of the season when I was there, but I just wasn't ready at the time."

"And all that 'Brock's a Crock' stuff, well that pissed me off too," he said. "But there was nothing I could do about it except continue to become the best quarterback that I could be and play hard."

"Look, I know that the quarterback gets a lot of the blame when the team loses and credit when they win. That's just the way the game is. Those last comments were made by someone who never took the time to get to know me or what I was all about. I'm not an easy person to talk to when I first meet someone because I'm shy and a little introverted. But those who really know me would never say those things, because I'm the complete opposite. It's also difficult to understand what a person is really like from afar. Being on the field wearing a helmet in the middle of a game or speaking in short sound bites at a press conference is not really a good way to get to know someone and what they're really like."

"Hell, I was the best quarterback in the league in both 1977 and 1978. In 1976, I was the second best passer in the league to Ronnie Lancaster and beat Lancaster all three times we played them. I had more wins than any quarterback in the league from 1976 to 1978 with twenty-nine. And because I was injured and missed a lot of games in 79, he's writing all this bull crap."

In a follow-up piece a few days later, Matheson wrote,

"I strode into Coach Jauch's office on Tuesday morning and asked him for details of the letter he got from his quarterback and his face lost all its colour and he almost fell off his chair. The last thing he wanted was a public forum on the letter and he asked me to forget the whole thing, which I refused to do, of course, advising him his wasn't the only competitive business in town."

The intent of Matheson's column was to make sure the situation became a public forum and in the same column, published Dieter Brock's home address in Birmingham.

"I did get a lot of letters. A lot!" recalls Brock. "But it backfired, because most of them were from fans saying they supported me and wanted me to come back to Winnipeg. Those were from the 'Diete's A Treat Fan Club.'"

All through the 1979 season, Ray Jauch had always been publicly supportive of his quarterback and had no intention of trading him regardless of what was being said. Brock had completed 1,069 passes for 14,389 yards and 88 touchdowns. He was within four completions of catching Blue Bombers' career passing leader, Ken Ploen and Jauch was confident that he had the quarterback he needed.

"I want to have some time to talk with him," Jauch stated to the media. "But I'd like to let things cool down a bit. There's no big rush; he's under contract. He's not the first player to say he's unhappy. It happens all over. I'm not that concerned about it right now."

In the Free Press, Larry Tucker, who had actually called Brock at his Birmingham home, wrote a more accurate piece on the subject. According to Tucker, Brock had said, "Things were frustrating for me this year. My knee got hurt and I kept stretching it. I just couldn't do the things I wanted to do."

"Then there were all the changes, especially on the offensive line," he continued in the interview. "At one point this year probably the only lineman left from the previous year was John Bonk."

"But it seems to me like everybody thinks I'm the reason we didn't win. I'm caught in all of it, because I've been here the longest. It all comes back to me."

On December 18, Ray Jauch signed a new contract with the Winnipeg Blue Bombers. Jauch had signed his original three year deal in 1978 and still had a year left when the club made the extension. They had agreed to extend their deal an extra year through 1981 to give him more time to turn things around.

General manager, Earl Lunsford had said the club was on the right track with Jauch and at the announcement he stated, "We were disappointed with the 1979 season naturally, but we think we're heading in the right direction and we think Coach Jauch is the man who'll take us there."

Jauch's response was, "I see no reason why we can't have the kind of winning football team that Winnipeg deserves."

Both men, when asked, had confidence that their starting quarterback would be back, healthy and motivated to win.

Unfortunately, being a celebrity, especially in a small market, means there is more than the usual assaults on one's ego when things don't work out the way others would like. The target can be vulnerable to the personal evaluations of other people who are far outside of the situation. Those on the receiving end have said the press can be relentless in trying to capture, then condemn, their celebrity prey and eventually with enough encouragement, the public seems to believe that they are ultimately in control of whether the career continues.

In January 1980, Jack Matheson made a prediction again in his column for the 1980 season. "The Blue Bombers will finish at 8-8 in the West, and the quarterback in October won't be Dieter Brock, more likely somebody they got from Ottawa for B. Ruoff."

"Ray did come down to Birmingham," said Brock. "We talked for quite a while and aired out a lot of things that been bothering both of us. I really didn't want to go anywhere else. Winnipeg was my team and I desperately wanted to win. And he felt the same way."

"We worked things out," said Brock. "And I was excited about the upcoming season."

"In the off-season, I went back to my workouts the way I'd always done it and even added some different types of routines to work on my throwing. I continued with the weighted ball throws and added some pulley work with a machine that you could tighten the tension to go through a throwing motion."

"I had more motivation than ever to get better because of what Ray had said to me," Brock recalled. "I wanted to make that year my best year ever. Yes, it did piss me off about how some of the fans had turned against me. But I knew the only way to deal with it was to ignore it and just go out and play and do the things you're supposed to do as the quarterback."

"As long as I was healthy, I had plenty of confidence in my ability," he said. "I had never lost confidence in my ability to throw the football."

A healthy Brock proved his worth on the first day of the Winnipeg Blue Bomber's Training camp. Coach Jauch had brought in rookies Mike Rieker and Jim Krohn in the off-season to compete for the back-up position, but it was obvious from the beginning that Brock was number one. Both rookies proved they could also throw the ball, which was a welcome change from the previous year and did a lot for the moral of the team.

"My knee felt good," he said. "But I started wearing a brace just in case. I wasn't going to take any chances.

Jauch decided to start Brock in their first pre-season game against the Alouettes. Rieker and Krohn would be put into the game later, splitting their time to see if they had potential in a game situation.

The Blue Bombers did a good job controlling the game against Montreal, but far too many penalties and fumbles contributed to a 26-20 loss. Neither rookie quarterback had gained ground with the coach. Jim Krohn was successful on one series, but he threw an interception which was returned for a touchdown. Rieker had problems holding the ball and he wasn't able to put points on the board.

Jauch decided to leave Krohn in Winnipeg on the team's Calgary trip to face the Stampeders. His intention was to play Brock for a full half and let Mike Rieker complete the game.

Winnipeg was able to take an early lead and was ahead 15-2 before the midway point of the second quarter. Brock saw most of the action in the first and fourth quarters. He went 10 of 19 on his passes, but young Rieker had issues moving the ball. He failed to put points on the board and was intercepted. He went 2-4 with a total offence of just four yards in the 25-23 loss.

In their third pre-season win, the Blue Bombers tried and succeeded on five third-down situations against the Argonauts. When a head coach let's his quarterback take charge in a third-down situation, it's a key indication of trust and confidence. Brock ran one himself, then used running back, Mark Bragagnolo to carry the ball over the scrimmage line. Jim Krohn was set to start in the second half, but when the Blue Bombers couldn't build up a lead, Jauch went right back to Brock, who went all out for the 20-16 victory.

In their 26-22 pre-season win against the B.C. Lions, Brock and Krohn shared the quarterbacking duties in the game. Krohn completed seven of ten passes for 93 yards during his second quarter time on the field. His lone touchdown march was 79 yards in seven plays and the pre-season ended with a 2-2 record.

There were high hopes when the team went into their first regular season game against the Eskimos. The Blue Bombers fought hard, but the result was a 36-13 loss. The lopsided score was by no means an indication of what actually happened on the field. The Birmingham Rifle threw for 450 yards in what was called a spectacular show.

His 450 yard performance tied the Winnipeg Blue Bombers' record for passing in a single game that was originally set by Don Jonas against the B.C Lions in 1971. Brock had also passed Ken Ploen's long standing record of 1,084 completions by a Blue Bomber quarterback.

But for Brock, it was team first and his performance was not a cause for celebration.

Even with the impressive numbers he had put up in the first regular season game, Mr. Matheson of the Winnipeg Tribune still wasn't satisfied and suggested in his column the following day that the Winnipeg Blue Bombers should hire Ken Ploen to babysit Brock. He also predicted the Blue Bombers would miss the play-offs, and General Manager Lunsford would be fired and replaced with Ray Jauch.

At Empire Stadium, against the B.C. Lions, Brock put on another show, but by the final whistle all he had to show for it was a measly 20-41 completion record and a third consecutive defeat for team. Eight of his incomplete passes were clear receptions that were dropped by his intended receivers.

After the 26-6 loss, Brock spoke to the media from the locker room. "Sure, it's disappointing to lose. But I know everyone's trying to do all they can. We lost this game and I'm part of this team too. We're all in this together."

"I remember I went to Coach Jauch after that third game," recalls Brock. "I just wanted to know if I was doing what he wanted me to do. I felt good because even though we weren't scoring, we were moving the ball. He was great. He was patient and he really helped."

After the game, Ray Jauch was quoted as saying, "I know these guys can catch the football. Again, we had our opportunities. I have a theory, one I haven't talked to the guys about, but I feel the guys are trying so hard that it's backfiring."

The only backfiring in the next game would come from the Calgary side of the field. The Blue Bombers grabbed an early 21-4 lead and held it until halftime. The Stampeders came back in the third quarter, but Brock directed a touchdown drive and the Blue Bombers were able to gain control of game and beat Calgary 35-18.

According to Jauch, it was Brock's game to win and at times he looked spectacular. Even Jack Matheson wrote "Brock was the catalyst, the leader, the master, and all that. I doubt he ever played a better game as a Blue Bomber."

On August 13 at Winnipeg Stadium, the Edmonton Eskimos once again proved far too much for the Blue Bombers. The now 1-4 Blue Bombers managed to hold their own against the CFL's only undefeated team until the later part of the second quarter. Despite the fact the Eskimos' starting quarterback, Tom Wilkinson was ineffective, back-up, Warren Moon took control and beat the Blue Bombers 30-17. Brock completed 24 of 45 passes, but was sacked seven times by an aggressive defence.

On August 20, at Ivor Wynne Stadium in Hamilton, the Blue Bombers posted an impressive 34-13 win against the Tiger-Cats. The teams were tied 10-10 at halftime, but the Winnipeg defence stopped any offensive attack the Hamilton team tried to put together.

That win was precisely what the Winnipeg Blue Bombers needed in order to forget the 1979 season and set the tone for the rest of the 1980 season.

In Regina the next week, Blue Bombers' linebacker and Winnipeg born, Leo Ezerins personally deflated the Roughriders with a late first quarter interception off quarterback John Hufnagel. Two plays later, Dieter Brock threw a perfect 19 yard touchdown pass to Mike Holmes and the Blue Bombers went on to a 24-16 victory.

Brock received help from his offensive line and all his receivers throughout the game and as a result, he moved past Ken Ploen to become the Winnipeg Blue Bombers' career leader in passing yardage with 16,533 in just six and half seasons. He finished the night with 20 completions of 35 attempts for 315 yards.

"I learned to love Ray Jauch's system," said Brock. "When he got the pieces together which included John Bonk, Nick Bastaja, Larry Butler, Bobby Thompson and Butch Norman on the offensive line, and William Miller, Mark Bragagnolo, and Dan Huclack as running backs, with Rick House, Joe Poplawski, Mike Holmes and Robert Woods as receivers, I felt we were finally ready offensively in 1980."

And they were ready. By mid-October, the Winnipeg Blue Bombers had gone on an eight game winning streak and Dieter Brock was the number one quarterback in the league. He was just 40 completions and 63 attempted passes away from beating Calgary legend, Peter Liske's single season record established in 1967.

At a time when Matheson's prediction was that Dieter Brock and Earl Lunsford should have been gone and Ray Jauch was supposed to be in the general manager's office, the Winnipeg Blue Bombers were being touted as the greatest team in CFL history. The team had a 9-4 record, a spot in the play-offs and could clinch second place in the Western Conference with a win against the upcoming Calgary Stampeders.

For the first time in many years, the Winnipeg Blue Bombers were being labeled a Grey Cup contender. Each week, as the wins added up, the level of poise and confidence in the team's locker room heightened as well.

And Dieter Brock wasn't just having a good year; he was dominating the entire league.

In the West Semi-Final, they made it look easy against the once dominating Calgary Stampeders, beating them, 32-14. Led by Brock, the Blue Bombers jumped out to a 21-0 first-quarter lead. They survived a furious Calgary comeback, but completely controlled the final quarter of the game for the victory. Running back, Bragagnolo scored two touchdowns in the opening quarter and added a third in the fourth.

Tom Cudney, a wide receiver for the Blue Bombers during the '80 season recalled the intensity and power that Brock had on the field. "I had caught a 40 yard pass from him in the game," recalled Cudney. "When I went back to the huddle to get the next play, I noticed blood all over my pants. I couldn't figure out where it had come from until I looked at my hands. The force of his throw had split the skin on my hands open and they were bleeding."

But things were different in Edmonton. The Eskimos came out hard and attacked from the beginning. The All-Star defence sacked Dieter Brock seven times and limited the Blue Bombers to just 219 yards in total offence, while Edmonton finished the game with 383 yards. Brock, under pressure all day, was only able to complete 14 of his 34 pass attempts for 221 yards. Warren Moon was good on 17 of his 33 attempts for 257 yards and Eskimo's kicker, Dave Cutler accounted for 16 points in the game.

The 1980 Winnipeg Blue Bombers season would end with a disappointing 34-24 loss to Edmonton in the Western Conference Finals. The Eskimos would go on to beat the Hamilton Tiger Cats the following week, 48-10 to win the 68th Grey Cup.

But in 1980, Dieter Brock became the league's premier passer. He established league records with 304 completions from 514 attempted passes. The Winnipeg Blue Bombers gained 4,252 yards on Brock passes, with 28 touchdowns and an amazingly low 12 interceptions.

Mid-way through the season Saskatchewan's Ron Lancaster had said, "Say what you want about Brock, but he's the best player in the country and there's no question about that. He has dominated this league like nobody has done since Peter Liske was quarterbacking in the late '60s."

On Thursday, November 20, 1980, just eight days shy of a year from when Matheson's first article had appeared, Dieter Brock stood on a podium in Toronto to receive the 1980 Shenley Award as the outstanding player of the Canadian Football League. And true to form, Brock spread the honour among his teammates. "Everybody contributed that year," he said. "We had some new linemen we'd picked up who gave us a lot more experience on the line. Having Joe Pop back helped a lot and we picked up a couple of good receivers to take the pressure off Mike Holmes."

"From that point on, I felt like we were just so consistent offensively. As long as we could keep everyone healthy, we had a chance. We had so many weapons that we were hard to stop. I thought Ray had finally put the pieces together on offence and I was even more confident going into the next season."

Chapter Twelve

Webster's defines fame as;

a: public estimation : reputation

b: popular acclaim : renown: a state of being widely acclaimed and highly honoured.

But what that definition fails to do is to provide a clear indication what fame is worth and the value it has for others.

In 1980, Dieter Brock had set new team and league records by ripping apart defences that would normally have put fear in the hearts and minds of most other quarterbacks. Out of 320 players on nine different teams, Brock was recognized for his performance with a Shenley Award as the league's most outstanding player.

With Brock healthy, motivated and confident, he was able to lead the Winnipeg Blue Bombers to within a few yards of final unseating the dominating Edmonton Eskimos in the Western Conference. And one can only imagine what his offence could have done to the Hamilton Tiger-Cats in the Grey Cup Championship that year.

His stock had definitely risen throughout the 1980 season and he was entering the option year of his three year contract. For some it was hard to imagine the Winnipeg Blue Bombers without the Birmingham Rifle in control.

"I didn't want to play out my option year," said Brock. "It wouldn't have been fair to everyone if I had to play another year knowing that I would have to leave at the end of the season. My heart wouldn't be in it."

Under Canadian Football League rules, Brock was obligated to play through his option year at his previous year's salary of $80,000 if his contract could not be renegotiated. If he refused to play, he was required to wait until his Winnipeg deal expired before playing anywhere else.

"I wasn't looking to become the highest paid player in the league," said Brock. "But I wanted to be paid what some of the other top players in the league were getting paid."

We sometimes forget that we only witness a short period of an athlete's entire career. The average career of a player in the Canadian Football League is just 3.5 years and Dieter Brock was going into his sixth season with the Winnipeg Blue Bombers. And that number doesn't include the ten years of high school and college playing that he had already endured just to get on the Blue Bombers' roster.

Most CFL player have off-season careers that they turn to, but in Brock's case, like many of the other top performing athletes, they use their off-season to improve themselves.

"My wife worked fulltime back in Birmingham," said Brock. "I had a home and a family to take care of so I had to take all that into consideration. And those commitments weren't going to stop when my career ended."

"I met Gil Scott through Nick Bastaja and Mark Bragagnolo," said Brock. "He was representing both of them and I remember meeting him when we were playing a game in Hamilton."

Since his early days in Birmingham, other than brief conversations with his father, Brock had always been left to make his own career decisions. With Gil Scott on board, it would be the first time Brock had sought professional guidance and representation.

"Agents negotiate hundreds of times with various teams," said Gil Scott. "A skilled negotiator will get his client the best financial deal he can. An athlete's expertise lies in their skill for the game. That's what they've focused on all their life and they have worked diligently on and off the field to achieve their success."

"An agent networks with general managers and other teams to find his client's worth," Scott continued. "It's pretty hard for an athlete to do that when they are focused on their skill and only for the team they currently play with."

"Gil seemed to know just about everybody in the league," said Brock. "I thought he was very knowledgeable about what was going on in the CFL and since he represented other players, he would know what they were getting paid. I really wanted someone I could bounce some things off of."

"I wasn't trying to break the bank of the Winnipeg Blue Bombers," Brock continued. "That was never my intention. I knew we were a community owned team. I really wanted to stay in Winnipeg because I knew how good of a team we had."

At the end of January 1981, twenty-seven sports reporters, three from each of the nine CFL cities voted Ray Jauch the league's Coach of Year by presenting him with the Annis Stukus Trophy.

"This is highly gratifying, but not totally satisfying," Jauch told the national media. "We had a good year in Winnipeg last season. I always thought we would have, even when we didn't win our first few games."

"I was convinced it was only a matter of giving our young players time to play together and learn to act as a unit," he continued. "But I cannot, as a head coach, say I'm satisfied. I won't be until we win a Grey Cup. That is how you measure success in this league."

The Winnipeg Blue Bombers were definitely a good team, ranked in the top three or four in the league. But the team was struggling financially like many other community owned CFL teams at the time. In 1980, they had lost approximately $680,000 putting their two year losses just shy of a million dollars.

As a community owned organization, the Winnipeg Football Club had to answer to their Board of Directors which consisted of Winnipeg Enterprises, the team's landlord and stadium owner, and a selection of business personalities from around the community.

On the opposite end, teams like the Montreal Alouettes and Hamilton Tiger-Cats were privately owned and operated. In 1980, Vancouver real estate mogul, Nelson Skalbania owned and controlled the Montreal Alouettes and he alone had the final say on financial and personnel issues. Toronto Maple Leaf's stakeholder, Harold Ballard controlled the Tiger-Cats.

In February, Gil Scott had his first meeting with Blue Bombers' general manager, Earl Lunsford during league meetings in Toronto. Scott and Brock never publically disclosed the dollar amount they were looking for during the early days of their negotiations with the team, but did state the quarterback was looking for a five year deal.

"Earl was always great to work with," said Scott. "He was a tough negotiator and a real man of integrity. I always took him at his word."

"Dieter's first and foremost concern was for his family and his future," Scott recalls. "That's all he had on his mind."

"I wanted my next contract to be the last," said Brock. "I wanted to finish my career in Winnipeg because as far as I was concerned, I still wasn't finished the job."

Brock wasn't the only Blue Bombers' player in the midst of contract negotiations. Thirteen other players, including Joe Poplawski, would be negotiating contracts prior to the start of the '81 season.

Lunsford was facing an extremely difficult off-season. It was his job, as directed by the football club's Board of Directors to keep costs at a minimum and raise revenues. The team set a goal of selling 20,000 season tickets prior to the regular season to tackle the lagging revenue issue, but by the end of February, sales had stalled at 15,000. They were averaging just five to six sales per day.

A planned Bomber Blitz aimed at selling Bomber Booster Passes at $25 was set to air on CKY TV. But, unfortunately, everyone preferred to watch the Edmonton Oilers beat the New York Islanders in the Stanley cup play-offs that evening and effort was a dismal failure.

They also tried selling $10,000 corporate sponsorships, but feel short with only six sold. That left the football club with no choice but to raise ticket prices by .50 to $1.50 depending on seat selection to help with the bottom line.

"We had two more meetings," said Brock. "I told them what I wanted. My figure was way up here and their number was way down there. There had to be something, somewhere in between we could agree on and I understood that."

Meanwhile, the Toronto Argonauts had agreed to pay their quarterback, Tony Adams in excess of $100,000 per year and Edmonton's back-up, Warren Moon had signed ten one year contracts at $100,000 per year with the Eskimos. Ottawa's Condredge Holloway was being paid $60,000 in 1980 and was asking for $75,000 for the 1981 season. Harold Ballard was offering Tom Clements $1.3 million over 5 years to lead the Hamilton offence and the Montreal Alouettes were looking at securing Vince Ferragamo from the Los Angeles Rams of the NFL for $400,000 per season.

In Winnipeg, running back William Miller, was contractually obligated to play two more seasons for the Blue Bombers, but insisted he would not return until he was paid $100,000 a year compared to the $80,000 he had received the previous year.

Under pressure, the Winnipeg Football Club's president, Joe Wilder, went public stating that Brock was demanding in excess of $300,000 per season and wanted a five year deal. The club was prepared to offer him $140,000 per year with no guarantees. It was also stated that contract negotiations could go through until March, 1982 when Brock's contract expired which meant he would have to play the '81 season under his old salary.

"It was hard on me and my family, waiting around and hearing some of the things that were being said in the media," said Brock. "I was trying to focus on my work outs and getting ready for the season, but when you don't know what the future holds, it makes things hard."

"It's difficult on these guys," said Gil Scott. "It's a whole different world when a player comes up here to play. They move their family to a new community for six months of the year. They are away from friends and family where they are known and supported."

By May 1, nothing had been worked out. The three privately owned teams, with more money to throw around, had all secured their high-priced quarterbacks. The only other team in the league capable of paying large dollars was Edmonton, but they had already locked up Warren Moon for the next nine years. As the days passed, Brock's bargaining power was slowly deteriorating.

With training camp looming, the Blue Bombers coaches were busy building two different playbooks for the season, one with Brock at the helm and one without.

The merchants at Crossroads Shopping Centre in Winnipeg's east end had posted a banner inside the mall where customers could come and sign their moral support for the quarterback. At the same time others were submitting letters to the editor of the local newspapers stating Brock wasn't worth the money or the effort.

"All the waiting hurt both of us. There were things that came out in Winnipeg about the negotiations and there were some things I said that didn't help a whole lot either. In a lot of cases, you don't get the chance to tell your side and the whole thing just builds up and gets extremely frustrating. But through it all, I was always hopeful."

Eleven days later, Dieter Brock and his agent settled for $1.1 million over five years. He had agreed to play with the Blue Bombers through the 1986 season for just under $220,000 per season.

"I never wanted to leave," said Brock. "The big thing for me right from the start was to look after my family and my future. I'd said it before; I never wanted to be the highest paid player in Canada. I just wanted what I thought I was worth."

As it turned out, signing their Shenley winning quarterback was the best sales tool the Blue Bombers had at their disposal. Two days after the announcement of his signing, season ticket sales jumped to an average of 75 per day.

Coach Jauch came into the '81 training camp knowing he had to improve the team's defensive system while maintaining the successful offensive plan if they were ever able to get past the Eskimos. But in the week preceding camp, offensive linemates Larry Butler and Butch Norman indicated they would not be returning to the team. Both were considering retiring from football.

"I have a barn to build, cattle to sell and a farm to run," said Larry Butler in an interview with the Winnipeg Free Press. Butler and his family had a farm back in North Carolina. "If I can work those things out, I'll be there."

Butch Norman had applied for a six-month leave of absence from the school district where he was employed, but had been denied. He was appealing the decision with the town council back in Luverne, Alabama and had to wait for the decision.

"I really liked Butch," said Brock. "Not just because he was from Alabama. He was 6' 5" and had really long arms and natural country boy strength and agility. He had the desire to never get beat and we needed that on the team."

"Butch was so good that he tried to do his job and help out everyone else," Brock said. "I remember our offensive line coach, Coach Rainsberger telling Butch to quit worrying so much about helping other people. That wasn't his responsibility."

"I know in the off-season Butch had decided to retire and he took a job in Luverne, Alabama. I got involved with Earl Lunsford in an effort to try to get Butch to come back. Earl had offered Butch a three year guaranteed contract which at the time was unheard of for an offensive lineman. When it still wasn't enough, I told Earl I would give up $20,000 a year off my contract just to get him back."

Several days later, Norman informed the team that his leave was again denied and he would not be returning.

The team opened training camp with Brock as the designated starter, while second year backup, Jim Krohn, would compete for his position with new comers Mike Kalasmiki and Reggie Ogburn.

Two practice sessions into training camp, the Blue Bombers coaches were revising their offensive game plans. They knew they would need quality replacements for Norman and Butler. Franky Smith, a massive import lineman was from the Kansas City Chiefs looked to be an ideal replacement. The 6' 7" 260 pound lineman was put at the end of the line with 6' 8" 317 pound Bobby Thompson.

In the team's first pre-season game against Saskatchewan, the offensive line broke down early and Brock was sacked hard.

"I don't really know what happened," Brock said. "I was winding up to throw the ball when someone got me in the ribs. I was in a great deal of pain and was taken for x-rays."

"I'm not satisfied with what I saw," Jauch had said after the 19-10 loss. "We will have to do something that's for sure. I'm not certain right now, but we'll have to do something."

In the next pre-season game, Brock was fitted with a flak jacket to protect his bruised ribs. The Eskimos were relentless, winning 25-16 and Jauch still wasn't happy with offensive line break downs.

In a loss of 28-18 against the B.C. Lions, Brock still showed his value with two long touchdown passes to Holmes and Poplawski. But he threw an interception which led to a Lions' touchdown one play later and the Blue Bombers recorded their third pre-season loss.

Just before their fourth pre-season game against the Stampeders in Calgary, Larry Butler quietly checked into the Calgary Inn and sixteen hours later he was on the line protecting his quarterback. "He got here and he hadn't worked out at all, but he didn't hurt us," Brock had said after the game.

In the 16-14 win against the Stampeders, Brock went 9 for 20 with 160 yards and 1 interception while Jim Krohn was 0 for 1 with an interception as well.

A few days later, before the start of the regular season, Jim Krohn was released from the team. He had thrown well, but was having mobility issues and was a victim of Jauch's final cuts.

In his place, the Blue Bombers acquired Mark Jackson from the Toronto Argonauts. Jackson, 27, had started twelve games for Toronto in the 1980 season and led all quarterbacks in rushing with 393 yards on 62 carries. He had completed 231 of 404 and had become the first

Argonaut quarterback to pass for over 3,000 yards since 1968.

"Jackson has the experience and gives us a little more as a backup," Jauch had said.

The Blue Bombers first regular season game against the Hamilton Tiger-Cats was definitely a quarterback show. Brock went 21 of 36 for 384 yards while the Tiger-Cats Tom Clements was 24 of 37 for 349 yards and a Hamilton win of 33-23.

But the 0-1 Blue Bombers played hard in Saskatchewan the following week. Brock led the Blue Bombers offence to score 10 points in the final four minutes as they finalized their first win of the season, 22-20 against the Roughriders. Larry Butler's solid performance in the game earned him the CFL's top lineman of the week honours.

"The best thing Larry does is his pass blocking," said Jauch at the press conference following the game. "I'm glad to see Larry coming back good. He should be even better next week."

The following week, the Blue Bombers hosted the Eskimos. "It wasn't even close," said Edmonton head coach, Hugh Campbell after the Blue Bombers beat his Eskimos 38-28. In the second quarter, Brock picked apart the former Grey Cup champion's defence to put 25 points on the board. He had hit Poplawski twice for touchdown passes. Warren Moon had started the game for Edmonton, but Wilkinson was sent in after Moon injured his shoulder.

Jauch praised Brock's play calling and his ability to read the Edmonton defence.

"We had certain plays we wanted to run against the defence and we recognized their alignments and the game plan the coaches made up worked perfectly," Brock told the media. He finished the game 20 of 30 with 320 yards.

That win put the Blue Bombers in a 2-1 tie with the Edmonton Eskimos in the Western Conference standings.

Two more wins would be added to the Blue Bombers' win column. On their visit to Toronto, the Blue Bombers beat the Argonauts, 21-18.

Against Montreal, Brock found openings all over the field. He threw 19 of 30 for 295 yards. By end of the first half Winnipeg led 32-2, finally ending the game with 58-2 win.

An 18-17 loss to Calgary and a 28-10 loss to Edmonton were put in the books before a 31-8 win against the Ottawa Rough Riders set their record at 5-3 for the season.

In September, the Blue Bombers would lose two in a row before posting a 46-10 win against the B.C. Lions.

After the B.C. victory, on October 1, the Canadian Football League weekly awards were announced and for the first time, three members of the same club received national recognition as the best in the league. Following their lopsided 46-10 win against the Lions, Brock, defensive halfback Vince Phason and offensive tackle Frankie Smith were recognized for their outstanding performances.

Brock had put together his best game of the season against the second place Lions. He completed 28 of 41 for 416 yards in passing offence. They managed to post a total offence of 570 yards.

"That guy was amazing," said Smith recalling his time with the Blue Bombers and his quarterback. "He was like my Momma back there. Nobody, and I mean nobody was ever allowed to hit my Momma."

"On the field and off, Diete was a stand-up guy with a big heart. No one ever knew that because he was so quiet," said Smith. "He gave me one of his cars to use when I got there because I couldn't afford one. I used it the whole time I was there."

Behind the scenes, assistant general manager Paul Robson was quietly making plans to secure yet another asset for the team's offensive line.

Unbeknownst to the Alouettes' rookie Chris Walby, he had been waived by the Montreal team.

Born in Winnipeg, Walby had grown up in the city's North End. He started playing junior football for the first time in grade 12, but his primary sport was hockey where he played defence for the Kildonan North Stars.

Competing from 1975 to 1977, Walby scored just four goals and nine assists on the ice, but managed to tally up 275 minutes in penalties. North End Winnipeg hockey was known for its tough style of play in the league and he fit in perfectly. It was really no surprise that Walby became involved in a pre-game fight during a playoff game and along with a teammate, they were both arrested in the dressing room in full equipment.

After his junior hockey career had ended, Walby started playing football with the Winnipeg Rods and would go on to earn an athletic scholarship to play college football at Dickinson State University in North Dakota.

Walby was drafted in the first round of the 1981 CFL Draft by the Montreal Alouettes and had played five games on the offensive line. Wrangling by the Montreal management over his contract left Walby without a valid contract and he was waived by the team.

"Legally, I couldn't talk to him," said Blue Bombers' Paul Robson. "League rules didn't permit that. So I called his father and I told him to tell Chris there would be a ticket home waiting for him at the Montreal airport if he was interested."

Robson greeted Walby at the airport and within 30 minutes of his arrival had signed him to the Blue Bombers.

On October 3, against the Ottawa Rough Riders, the Blue Bombers celebrated their head coach's 10th anniversary in the CFL with a resounding 44-24 victory.

The entire game centered around Brock's stunning performance. He picked the Rough Riders' defence apart by completing 41 passes on 47 attempts for 449 yards. Never before in CFL history had a quarterback performed better.

"That was one of my most memorable games," said Brock. "Everything came together for the entire team."

True to form, following his amazing performance, Dieter Brock presented the game ball to Ray Jauch.

And because of that performance, Brock grabbed his third, and second straight CFL offensive player of the week honour.

"I think it's in him to do better every year," Coach Jauch had stated about his quarterback. "He understands the game better this year. He's making decisions a little quicker and using his backs a lot more."

And he did improve. The Blue Bombers would go undefeated in the month of October beating Toronto, B.C and Montreal, giving them a 10-5 record.

In their last game of the month, after four weeks with the team, Chris Walby finally saw game action with his new team. The result was a fumble recovery and Walby's first and only touchdown against his former team, the Montreal Alouettes.

Going into their final game of the season against Calgary, the Blue Bombers had already secured a spot in the playoffs. But Brock still went on, holding nothing back and passing for 122 yards, beating the Stampeders, 44-6.

He finished the season with 4,796 yards beating Sam Etcheverry's previous mark by 63 yards. Following the game, Brock spoke to media. "Of all the records, that was the one that was the hardest to achieve. You have to stay free of injury and play pretty well in every game. But I think it's more of a team accomplishment than one for me personally."

Dieter Brock's unprecedented passing for the season also provided Winnipeg's Eugene Goodlow his own record of being the first receiver in the CFL to grab 100 receptions in a single season.

In their Western Conference semi-final against B.C., the Lions' defence were able to take away two key pieces of the Bombers' offensive success. They were able to break through the Blue Bombers' offensive line and they stayed focused on getting to the Birmingham Rifle's receivers. The Lions' strategy worked, eventually defeating the Blue Bombers is a tight 15-11 loss.

Brock had been able to pick apart the Lions defence during their 46-10 and 49-12 victories in the regular season, but was sacked five times in the semi-final game.

On the Blue Bombers final drive of the game, they showed promise as the offence faced a second and nine at the Winnipeg 51 yard line with 90 seconds left. As Brock cocked his arm back to throw, the Lions defence rushed in and knocked the ball out of his hand and the Winnipeg Blue Bombers' 1981 season came to an end.

They finished the season in second place in the Western Conference with an impressive 11-5 record.

Brock's 1981 accomplishments included 354 completions in 566 attempts for 4, 796 yards, all new CFL records at the time. He finished the season with 32 touchdown passes and just 15 interceptions.

Three weeks after the team's heartbreaking loss against B.C., Dieter Brock was presented with his second consecutive Shenley Award as the CFL's outstanding player. The moment held some satisfaction because he stood on the Montreal stage with teammates, Larry Butler, chosen top offensive lineman and Joe Poplawski who was honoured as the top Canadian.

The only thing more satisfying for the Birmingham Rifle would have been to stand with his entire team and accept the Grey Cup.

Chapter Thirteen

The best laid schemes o' Mice an' Men
Gang aft agley, (often go awry)
An' lea'e us nought but grief an' pain,
For promis'd joy!

In his 1768 poem, To A Mouse, Robert Burns tells of how the narrator, while ploughing a field, cuts through a mouse's nest. The poet shows regret and apologizes to the mouse. The implication is that even when you mean no harm and have pure intentions, you can destroy somebody else's well laid plans.

Today, we often use the phrase "Murphy's Law," which also means, regardless of how well one is organized and prepared, sometimes unforeseen obstacles can get in the way.

In 1982, Ray Jauch's training camp fell short of everyone's expectations because of bad weather, player holdouts and injuries throughout the entire month of May. "We haven't had much contact in our training camp," Jauch had said to the media. With the weather damaged field and lack of players, the coaching staff did not have the opportunity to evaluate their entire roster as well as they had intended.

Supposedly, Larry Butler and Earl Lunsford had spoken in early January about his return to the team. Butler had offered to accept an identical deal to the one he had in 1981, which included a guaranteed salary. The issue was that the Blue Bombers had changed their stance on guaranteed contracts and were no longer granting them.

Butler, whose wife was eight months pregnant, wasn't sure things could be worked out. "I just can't get up and move 2,500 miles with a wife and two kids," he was quoted as saying. "I'd need somebody to look after my farm, also."

Chris Walby was the early leader to take over for Butler, but he lacked the experience that Butler had amassed.

In March, back-up quarterback Mark Jackson had agreed to a two year contract. He had finished the '81 season with 37 completions on 52 attempted passes for 435 yards and was comfortable in Jauch's offensive system.

The team's big test would have to be their first pre-season game against the Calgary Stampeders. Brock would be splitting the duties with Jackson and newcomer, Steve Pisarkiewicz who had been picked up in the off-season to compete with Jackson for the back-up position.

Jauch used all sixty players during the game because of the lack of training camp exposure. Brock and the other two quarterbacks had a total of eleven different receivers available to them.

Pisarkiewicz was helped off the field after being hit by Calgary linebacker, Deacon Nausler, but the Bombers pulled off an easy 22-0 victory.

Back in Alabama, the Alabama Sportswriters Association announced Ralph Dieter Brock as their top professional athlete of the year. Brock had beaten out NASCAR driver, Bobby Allison, New England Patriots all-pro guard, John Hannah, New York Mets, George Foster, New York Jets quarterback, Richard Todd and Kansas City Kings forward, Reggie King for the honours.

Because Brock was in the middle of the team's preseason schedule, Alabama Governor, Fob Jones flew to Winnipeg to make the presentation at the Blue Bombers office.

After beating the B.C. Lions, 25-11 and the Saskatchewan Roughriders, 25-16, the Blue Bombers had the best Western Division pre-season record. The Blue Bombers were unbeaten in three outings with the Roughriders second best at 2-3.

Against the Roughriders, Brock was forced into action when Mark Jackson suffered a concussion and Steve Pisarklewicz took a hard hit that left him unable to continue.

Six days later, in their final pre-season game against the Edmonton Eskimos, Mark Jackson started the game, but had difficulty moving the ball. Brock was sent in again and went 16-31 for 201 yards, but the result was Blue Bomber first and only pre-season loss.

Right from the start of training, everyone in the Winnipeg organization knew the daunting task ahead was to unseat the Edmonton Eskimos. The four time Grey Cup Champions showed no signs of slowing down and Winnipeg had been the victim of a 20 year Grey Cup drought.

The Blue Bombers' regular season opened at home against the Saskatchewan Roughriders. Kicker Trevor Kennard opened the 1982 season with 18 points, five field goals, two converts and a single. The final score was 31-21. For the first time in Jauch's five years as the Blue Bombers' Head Coach, his opening day record was 1-0.

The second game was against the new Montreal Concordes. The Concordes were formed just two weeks before the CFL training camps opened as a replacement for the Alouettes, who were forced to shut down operations because of financial issues. The Montreal team had not only lost its identity, but they lost their million dollar talent as well. Players like Vince Ferragamo, Billy Johnson and James Scott all returned to the National Football League.

Winnipeg moved the ball with ease in the first half with 307 yards of offence. At the final whistle, Brock finished the game with 382 passing yards.

The Blue Bombers defence took no pity and shut down the Concordes offence while Brock and his weapons rang up an impressive 36-0 win inside the quiet Olympic Stadium.

It was hard for Jauch to find fault with such a lopsided win, but he was concerned with the lack of protection on his quarterback. "Brock got rid of the ball, but he still got hit," Jauch stated a few days after the game. "That concerns me."

Against the Hamilton Ticats, the Blue Bombers took an early 21-7 halftime lead. After a Brock interception, Ticats quarterback, Tom Clements stormed back with 21 fourth quarter points to win the game 36-25.

Prior to the Hamilton game, Brock had gone six consecutive regular season games without throwing an interception.

Behind the scenes, rumours started circulating about a weekend meeting between Ray Jauch and John Bassett. Bassett owned the Tampa Bay franchise of the new United States Football League and had made it public that he wanted Ray Jauch to lead his new team.

Jauch had three years remaining on his Blue Bomber's contract, although like all CFL coaches, his contract gave him the rights to accept a better offer should one become available.

Out west, the Eskimos Head Coach, Hugh Campbell's name was also popping up in conversations about the USFL.

On August 1, the Blue Bomber offence ripped apart the Edmonton secondary in the opening thirty minutes of the game as Brock threw for 275 yards. On the other side of the line, the Bombers' defence shut down Warren Moon's running and tightly covered his receivers. The Winnipeg club went on to win 32-26 and put the Blue Bombers into a first place tie with the B.C. Lions in the Western Division.

Six days later, the Lions left Winnipeg with a 29-16 loss, leaving the Bombers sole leaders in the division.

On August 17, Dieter Brock and family welcomed daughter, Meredith McKenzie who was born in Winnipeg.

Two days later, the new father pummelled the Calgary Stampeders in the first quarter by giving his team a 17-0 lead. Brock opened the game with 12 straight completions including a 75 yard touchdown pass to William Miller and a 51 yard toss to Eugene Goodlow. Brock finished the game with 22 completions on 37 attempts for 364 yards.

That win was the Blue Bombers fifth in six regular season games and put them three points ahead of Calgary in the top spot of the Western Division.

On August 24, the Winnipeg Football Club hastily called a press conference at their Maroon's Road office. Earl Lunsford stepped up to the microphone and announced that Ray Jauch would be leaving the organization at the end of the '81 season. The Blue Bombers' head coach had agreed to coach the USFL's Washington Federals. His new three year contract was worth $150,000 per year. Jauch had spent 19 seasons in the CFL and the last seven with the Winnipeg club. He was the fifth winningest coach in CFL history with 110 victories.

"Earl Lunsford told the press that Ray was leaving for the Washington Federal's," said Brock. There had been rumours, but this was a real shock. We found out the same way everyone else did. I was disappointed because we had such a good team that year. I thought, just like the Bud Riley firing, here we go again. We would be starting over with a new coach, a new system with more changes and unknowns. I tried not to dwell on it too long, because we were having such a good year."

Also expected to be heading south to the new league was the Saskatchewan Roughriders GM, Jim Spavital, Edmonton's Hugh Campbell and Calgary coach, Jack Gotta.

With the disappointing news still circling around the team, it was hard for anyone to expect a win in their next game. But they did win. Ottawa fell to the Blue Bombers by a score of 27-20 and seemed like it was business as usual.

Running back William Miller, ran for 213 yards against the Saskatchewan Roughriders the following week in a hard fought 36-35 win. Brock had also run for two touchdowns, but was sacked four times. He was the first to admit that he wasn't sharp. After the game he spoke to media. "I didn't feel comfortable. It's nice to have a 7-1 record, but if you lose a game, somebody will be right behind you."

"We were really good offensively, averaging well over 30 points a game," said Brock. "But the injury to Eugene

Goodlow during game six really hurt us. Goodlow had caught 30 balls for over 500 yards and eight touchdowns in five games. He was on pace to catch well over 20 touchdowns. And then we lost Mike Holmes as well. He had 35 catches and over 400 yards when he went out."

The struggle continued as the Blue Bomber offence was ineffective against the Stampeders in the following game. The Calgary pass rush proved too much for the offensive line while the Stampeders' secondary closely covered Brock's receivers. The result was a 15-11 loss, putting the Blue Bombers' season at 7-2 and just one point ahead of the second place Stampeders.

The Blue Bombers' chaulked up another loss against the Ottawa Rough Riders on September 18. The offensive line got pounded, leaving Brock little time to throw. Opponents had started to double cover the Bombers' inside receivers, shutting down Rick House and Joe Poplawski.

It seemed like the team Ray Jauch had spent years building was starting to fall apart. The once promising season was becoming a year of frustrated hope for the coach and his players.

In the next game, they were barely able to squeeze out a victory against the visiting Montreal Concordes. Brock was able to pull things together in the last four minutes to get close enough for a 52 yard field goal by Trevor Kennard.

"I don't know what the problem is," said Brock after the game. "I know we've got to play a lot better than we did tonight to beat better teams.

In early October, Dave Supleve of the Winnipeg Free Press published an article with the headline "Brock longs for 1 home." The article went on to state that Brock longed for the opportunity to perform in front of his hometown. His desire had intensified with the emergence of the United States Football League and one of its 12 charter members, the Birmingham Stallions.

"I think it's only natural for a player to want to play in his hometown," Brock was quoted. He was now 30 years old, in his ninth season as a Winnipeg Blue Bomber and in the second year of his five year contract.

A move to the USFL could only be arranged if Brock could convince the Blue Bombers' general manager, Earl Lunsford to free him from the remaining four years of his contract, but Lunsford had stated publically that he would not renegotiate the contracts of any player.

It made the situation even more difficult when Brock's wife, Kathy had returned to Birmingham with their children in August for the start of school. Brock admitted the life of a bachelor added an emotional strain on his life.

"This is a great contract I have here in Winnipeg," said Brock in the interview. "And this isn't a ploy to have it renegotiated. I'm not even thinking about it. I'm only concerned about turning this team around. I'm not even concerned about next year."

After the Blue Bombers 29-17 victory against the B.C. Lions the following week, Brock said, "It looks like we're coming out of a slump."

Nine days later, he threw four touchdown passes to lead the Blue Bombers to another win against Toronto. With all the protection he needed, his receivers found space giving him time to complete 19 of 30 attempts for 268 yards.

In a rematch against the Argonauts in Toronto the following week, Brock was having his best game of the season, going 17 of 21 for 269 yards. But Toronto's defensive tackle Leon Lyszkiewicz managed to break through the offensive line and leveled the quarterback with two minutes remaining in the first half. Brock laid still on the turf of Exhibition Stadium for almost two minutes while Jauch paced the sidelines.

Eventually he was helped off the field leaving Ray Jauch no other choice. After eleven months of watching from the sidelines, backup Mark Jackson was sent in and the Bombers managed to hold on for a 29-10 win.

The following week against Edmonton, Brock spent the final three quarters of game on sidelines after taking a vicious hit to the ribs. Jackson stepped in again, but this time the Eskimos dominated the game and took the victory. The 33-17 loss put the Blue Bombers at 11-4, going into a two week break.

After four relatively healthy seasons, injuries were starting to wear on Brock. A month earlier, it was a sprained thumb on his throwing hand and now a swollen right wrist, damaged rib cartilage and a stiff back were all taking their toll on him. The break helped him heal while spending a few days back in Birmingham.

"I had a lot of small injuries that year," said Brock. "It was getting frustrating."

Their final game of the regular season was against Hamilton. Tiger-Cats' Tom Clements needed just three completions and 162 yards passing to break two of Brock's year old passing records. But Clements would not last the game. He was taken to the hospital for x-rays after taking a hit and coughing up blood in the locker room. Back-up Dave Marler was called in and directed the Tiger-Cats to a 24-21 victory over the Bombers.

The loss put the Blue Bombers in second place in the Western Division behind the Edmonton Eskimos and forced an upcoming semi-final game against the Calgary Stampeders.

In Edmonton's final game, quarterback Warren Moon needed 341 yards to reach 5,000 and he got exactly that with 21 completions in 32 attempts, including three touchdowns. Brock had held the record of 4,795 from the previous season.

In their semi-final matchup with Calgary, the Blue Bombers held the Stampeders to just one field goal in the 24-3 win. But despite the lopsided win, the Blue Bombers performance was not impressive and there was concern going into the Western final against the Eskimos.

In frigid -18C conditions, the Edmonton Eskimos proved why they had been four time winners of the Grey Cup. In the first half, Warren Moon picked apart the Blue Bombers defence for a halftime lead of 17-9.

The Blue Bombers last drive of the season would be a heroic effort from their own 18 yard line with 31 seconds left to play. Brock, in a last desperate attempt, threw a bomb to Nate Johnson, but the ball was knocked away by Edmonton safety Mike McLeod.

After the game, a frustrated Brock refused to speak to the media. Like so many of his teammates, his disappointment said everything.

"Our players deserved to win," Coach Jauch had said following his final game as a member of the Winnipeg Blue Bombers. "I think Edmonton also deserved to win. It's a shame both of us can't be around for the final day."

"That was another heartbreaking loss," said Brock. "We really believed that we finally had the team that could win it all. The Eskimos had had their run and now it was supposed to be our turn. I know we got James Murphy later on for the playoffs and James was going to be a great receiver, but it takes time to develop confidence in new guys."

"We lost 24-21 because of missed passes and field goals. I think we missed four field goals. There was a couple of penalties that killed us, one in particular. We are just taking the lead 21-18 when Warren Moon started rolling to his right and was intercepted by Charles Williams. We would have had great field position, but the refs called a roughing the passer penalty on John Helton. That was very questionable call."

The Winnipeg Blue Bombers would go another year as the most hopeful team in the league, but with the longest Grey Cup absence in the CFL.

"It was after the season was over when I was home and away from all that that I really started thinking about Ray Jauch leaving," recalled Brock. "Ray really was my favourite. I have a great deal of respect for him. I always will."

"I don't think I would have considered leaving if Ray had stayed," Brock said. "But now we were going to get a new coach and we were all going to have to start over. I just kept thinking more changes and uncertainty. And was I going to fit in with what little time I had left?"

Still, thou art blest, compar'd wi' me!
The present only toucheth thee:
But Och! I backward cast my e'e,
   On prospects drear!
An' forward tho' I canna see,

I guess an' fear!

If ever a poet understood the character of a person, it was Robert Burns. Even though he wrote in Scots or old English, the language he was most fluent in was the language of the heart. All too human in his personal life, he had the ability to put truth onto the page. Nothing was too small or too large to escape his notice, from a mouse in the mud to a God in his heavens, Burns used his words to speak to us, soul to soul.

His creation of that stanza in the opening of this chapter could very well be a fitting description for what Dieter Brock had endured in the '82 season.

But it's Burn's last stanza of that poem that has even more meaning to the situation. In the poem, the narrator, unlike the mouse, casts his focus on the past rather than looking to the future. And unlike the mouse who lives in the present, guesses and fears for what the future might hold.

Chapter Fourteen

On Friday Dec 3, 1982 just a few weeks after the team's disappointing loss against the Edmonton Eskimos in the Western Finals, Winnipeg Blue Bombers' General Manager, Earl Lunsford stepped down after 15 years with the organization.

Frustration was something Lunsford had put up with on almost a daily basis from a city that desperately wanted a championship. Over the years there were "Trade Lunsford" bumper stickers and "Earl Must Go" signs throughout the city. Petitions calling for his dismissal were common at the team's head office. After fifteen years of taking the heat, Lunsford had had enough.

Four days after his resignation, the Board of Directors announced that Assistant General Manager, Paul Robson, would be moving up to succeed Lunsford.

A native of Winnipeg, Robson had spent eighteen years with the club, first as a linebacker and centre and then the last eight as the Assistant General Manager and Director of Player Personnel. Robson's first priority was obvious; to find a new head coach for the team.

Unfortunately, the United States Football League, a new league that had been established, had started pillaging the front offices and coaching ranks of the Canadian Football League as well as the National Football League. The USFL was scheduled to start their inaugural season in the spring of 1983 and had been actively recruiting management, coaches and player personnel since early 1982.

The concept behind the USFL had actually been conceived back in 1965 by New Orleans businessman,

David Dixon. Dixon had seen an opening for another professional football league that would play in the United States during the summer, when the National Football League and college leagues were in their off-season. Their scheduling would be in direct competition with the CFL.

The USFL team's had no hard salary cap, and because of that, teams quickly escalated player payrolls in an effort to fill their ranks with quality talent. As some owners began engaging in bidding wars for personnel and players against NFL and CFL teams and each other, they forced other owners to do the same or face a competitive disadvantage.

But on January 25, 1983, the Winnipeg Blue Bombers announce they had secured Cal Murphy as the team's new head coach. The timing was impeccable and his football credentials were impressive. Murphy had been the offensive line coach with the Edmonton Eskimos under head coach Hugh Campbell. Like Ray Jauch, Campbell had left after 1982 for the USFL as the head coach of the league's Los Angeles Express.

Under Campbell and Murphy, the Eskimos had won an unprecedented five straight CFL titles with star quarterbacks like Tom Wilkinson and Warren Moon. Those same Eskimos had beaten the Blue Bombers 24-21 in the '82 West Division Finals just two months before the announcement.

In his early days, Murphy had attended Vancouver College where he had been a football standout. He then moved on to play with the University of British Columbia Thunderbirds as a left-handed quarterback and defensive back as well as a brief stint with the BC Lions in 1956. Murphy then took over the reins at UBC as the Thunderbirds head coach in 1960-61. He led the team to their only undefeated season.

Following that, Murphy became the assistant coach at Eastern Washington University under Head Coach Dave Holmes. He followed Holmes to the University of Hawaii Rainbows, and became part of the most successful coaching tenure in Hawaii history. In 1973, Murphy left

Hawaii for the San Jose State Spartans to work under head coach Darryl Rogers.

Cal Murphy joined the CFL coaching ranks in 1974 with the BC Lions under head coach Eagle Keys, and became head coach after six games in the 1975 season. He was fired after the 1976 season and moved on to spend the 1977 season with the Montreal Alouettes under head coach Marv Levy.

In 1978, Murphy took a job as offensive line coach with the Edmonton Eskimos under head coach Hugh Campbell and remained there until joining the Blue Bombers in 1983. His appointment was a bit of a homecoming as Murphy was born in Winnipeg in 1932. His football career seemed to have now come full circle.

Murphy stressed at the team's announcement that he felt the area that hurt the Blue Bombers more than anything in the previous season was losing their starting outside receivers. Eugene Goodlow had suffered an injury midway through the season, and then eventually left to sign with the New Orleans Saints in the NFL. Mike Holmes never fully recovered from his injury, a torn Achilles, which kept him out late in 1982 and was now on the roster of the USFL's Washington Federals with Ray Jauch.

But Murphy did see a positive with his new team. He claimed that Dieter Brock was an "awfully formidable weapon."

While the new coach settled into his new office and familiarized himself with his new team, rumours of the USFL still haunted the Canadian league. It was reported that many high profile CFL imports were anxious to join the USFL as soon as possible.

Names like Argos running back Cedric Minter and quarterback Condredge Holloway were being pursued. Others like receivers Tom Scott and Brian Kelly of the Eskimos, quarterback Mark Jackson and receiver Rick House from the Blue Bombers and Hamilton Tiger-Cats linebacker, Ben Zambiasi were also being pursued.

Zambiasi was reported as saying, "If the USFL existed when I came out of college, I'm sure I would have opted for the USFL instead of the CFL. I think fans will see a noticeable deterioration in the calibre of the CFL, not as much this year, but eventually."

While some of the USFL contracts for players like Herschel Walker at $5 million over three years and Reggie Collier's four year deal at $2.3 million were being admired, the reality of the situation was quite different. The average USFL annual salary was in the $25-30,000 range while the CFL's average was slightly higher at $49,000 per season and the NFL's average was $90,000.

"Money wasn't always the motivating factor for an import player," said agent, Gil Scott. "It's quite expensive for an American player to move his family for six months of the year. There's also the appeal of playing to a bigger audience and in some cases in front of your own hometown."

Blue Bombers back-up quarterback Mark Jackson had said in an interview that he had talked to several teams in the USFL.

"I would have had a pretty good opportunity with three or four teams," the 28 year old Jackson had said in an interview. "We tried, but there's nothing they're (the Blue Bombers) willing to do. I can't control my own destiny." Paul Robson had turned down Jackson's request to end his relationship with the team.

"The Blue Bombers hold all the cards. I'm sure they're not going to start a trend by letting people go so they can change leagues," Jackson had said.

The Blue Bombers had decided to take a hard stance on Jackson after the 1982 rumour had circulated about Brock heading to the USFL's Birmingham Stallions if he could be released.

Paul Robson again stated that the club's position would not change when it came to letting players out of their contracts. But just when the rookie general manager thought that the issue had been closed for good, a larger one opened.

On April 28, the Winnipeg Football Club made an official announcement that shook the city of Winnipeg and the entire league.

"The Winnipeg Football Club regrets to announce it has received a letter of retirement from quarterback Dieter Brock."

It seemed that after nine seasons, The Birmingham Rifle was finished. "I wrote a letter to the Bombers explaining that I'm retiring from the Winnipeg Football Club," Brock had stated.

"I don't know where I'll go from here," Brock had said in a telephone interview from his home in Birmingham with Dave Supleve from the Winnipeg Free Press. "I'm very serious about what I'm doing. But I don't know when I'll play again."

"I didn't want leave the team, right away," said Brock. "I was just hoping to have some discussions about shortening my contract, but nobody would listen to me. They wouldn't even talk about it."

Unless someone somewhere had a sudden change of heart, the Winnipeg Blue Bombers were going to have to say goodbye to their two-time Shenley Award winning quarterback.

And then, all hell broke loose. Dieter Brock went from hero to villain in just a few headlines and sound bites. For the next three months, speculation, rumors and innuendos fueled not just the Winnipeg media but also the entire country.

"Dieter Brock wants more money." "Brock wants to be traded." "He is joining the Ray Jauch in USFL." "He's fishing with a friend at Lake of the Woods," were just some of the insinuations and accusations that were being made almost on a daily basis in the Winnipeg media. On one occasion, there were two different stories on the same page of the same newspaper claiming he was in two different locations.

"I had no idea all that was going on up there," said Brock. "I was home in Birmingham with my family and remember, those were the days when there was no email, online news or Google."

"But I can tell you; it wasn't a matter of trying to get more money from the Blue Bombers or to go anywhere else in the CFL. I never wanted to play for any other team in the

CFL. I never asked to get out of my contract. I just wanted it shortened."

"Unless you play the game, it's hard for anyone to understand," he explained. "I felt we had a really good team when Bud Riley was fired. Then Ray was hired and he cleaned house. Yes, he developed a team that was ready to win it all, but everyone saw that it takes time. Then he leaves and now we have to go through the whole process again with a new coach. I felt like, oh no, here we go again."

"I wanted to play another year with the Bombers, but when they refused to even listen to me, I had no choice but to send my retirement letter."

"With the new league starting up, I felt that if I'm going to have to start all over again, I might as well try to do it somewhere closer to home. I knew I only had a few years left in my career and the thought of playing closer to home was really enticing."

When it came right down to it, it wasn't about the money, the USFL or even the NFL. It was about going home. It was about living and working in a place where Brock felt comfortable and known. In the nine years Brock had been with the Blue Bombers, he had moved his family more than twenty times.

"Yes, I was being paid well, but the cost of travelling and maintaining two homes in two different countries and making that move takes its toll."

"My wife would have to leave in the middle of August every year to get the kids in school," he said. "Financially, we were doing okay, that wasn't the issue, but sometimes it felt like we were only a part-time family. We were apart more than we were together."

"Other than John Bonk, I had been with the Bombers the longest of anyone on the team. We had gone through all those changes with two different coaches and now a third was coming in. My winning percentage as the quarterback was better than any other quarterback in the league except for the Eskimos who had the same general manager and the same coach for all those years. I felt at least I deserved the opportunity to talk about my future."

The seemingly endless barrage of Brock attacks in the media and public continued through the spring as the Blue Bombers prepared for the upcoming season. With training camp just weeks away, rookie head coach, Cal Murphy, had to get a team ready to hit the field.

"Right now, the way we're going, Mark (Jackson) has the experience and has been a starting quarterback in the league. We're going into camp with him as our number one quarterback," Murphy told the media.

In the back-up position, the Blue Bombers had their eye on Nicky Hall, a 25 year old quarterback from New Orleans. But Hall, who had been mentored by Archie Manning, wasn't ready to settle for a number two spot.

"The job is wide open now," he had stated after hearing of Brock's retirement. "I'm looking for a starting job. I never think of myself as being No. 2. You have to figure you're going to be No.1."

Norman Gibbs of Southern University had also been invited to the Bombers camp.

Cal Murphy opened the 1983 Winnipeg Blue Bombers training camp with plenty of new faces looking to make an impression. Almost every player that entered training camp was unsure of their future. There were, after all, just 38 positions up for grabs, four of which had to be held in reserve. Nineteen spots were available to non-import players on a team's active roster and just fifteen for the imports.

Gone from the 1982 roster along with Brock were running back William Miller, wide receiver Eugene Goodlow, defensive tackle John Helton and defensive backs Vince Phason, Charles Williams and Gregg Butler.

"I don't think anyone knew what to think of Cal Murphy at first," recalls second year offensive lineman, Lyle Bauer. "But what we found out early in camp was that it didn't matter who you were or what you had done. In his eyes, you were going to have to earn your spot on his team and he made that clear from day one. It was his team. It was his way or you weren't going to be around."

"From day one Cal made it obvious it was team first," said Bauer's linemate, Chris Walby. "You always had to fight for your spot. Cal always brought in guys to compete for your spot. The competition was fierce. Nothing was guaranteed with that guy. There was no loyalty from Coach Cal at first, but he most definitely demanded it from us."

"It didn't take long, that's for sure," said Bauer who now laughs at those early days. "Cal beat the shit out of us in training camp, physically and mentally. He was the exact opposite of Ray Jauch. We hit 'til we bled and ran 'til we puked, twice a day."

"Camp Calsky" was the name given by players during training camp. It was a tribute to the tough hauling they had gone through. "After camp was over, we had T-shirts made that said "I Survived Camp Calsky," said Bauer.

By the time Murphy had finished his first Winnipeg Blue Bombers' training camp, the total roster turnover from the 1982 season was thirty-two players.

On Friday June 10, Cal Murphy's Blue Bombers took the field in their first pre-season game against the Calgary Stampeders. Mark Jackson had originally been the designated starter, but an injured foot left him on the sidelines for Nicky Hall. Norman Gibbs and newcomers, Brian Broomell and Lawerence McCullough, who had also been brought, would see limited action at the quarterback position. The result was 20-4 loss to the Stampeders and all four quarterbacks failed to make a positive impression on their new coach.

It had been six weeks since Brock announced his retirement from the team and Paul Robson stated to the Free Press, "I haven't heard from Brock and I don't plan to call him."

One Free Press reporter stated that Brock and his family were vacationing in Florida while another wrote that he was preparing to seek his fortune with Ray Jauch and the Washington Federals of the USFL.

"I can tell you this," said Ray Jauch in a recent telephone interview. "I had not spoken to Dieter since I left the Blue Bombers. I wouldn't even think of it because he was under contract with them."

"It seemed like some Winnipeg sport writers wanted to blame me because we hadn't won the Grey Cup," said Brock. "It was just ridiculous."

After a close 24-23 loss to the B.C. Lions, the Blue Bombers faced the Edmonton Eskimos in their third pre-season game. The offence struggled again, posting just 71 yards in the opening half with the final result being the team's third straight pre-season loss of 34-16.

Blue Bomber receiver, Rick House stated after the game that, "There's no doubt that was very disheartening. There just doesn't seem to be any community out there. Our offence has lots of work to do."

Things didn't improve the following week as they fell 33-10 against the Saskatchewan Roughriders. Now 0-4 in the pre-season, with just days until the regular season started, Cal Murphy had far too many concerns with his offence.

"I was sitting in a restaurant in a hotel in Dallas when Dieter called and told me Robson was coming down to talk to him," Brock's agent Gil Scott recalled. "I remember it well. The Commodores were at the table next me."

"I jumped on a flight to Birmingham immediately," said Scott. "And we met with Robson at the Hilton for two days and tried to go through the issues."

"We didn't really solve anything," said Brock. "But he kept saying something to the effect that they would work something out if I came back to play. At first I wasn't comfortable with that."

"When we were in Birmingham, Robson said if Dieter came back up to Winnipeg to play, he would do something about the length of the contract," said Scott. "He promised."

But Robson returned to Winnipeg, disappointed. "I restated the position of the football club, in that we felt he would be required to play out the entirety of his contract," he stated at a press conference. "His position is the same. He insists he will not be playing with Winnipeg this year."

Three days later, on the eve of the Blue Bombers' opening regular season game, Gil Scott walked into the

Blue Bomber's office with his client. After a lengthy meeting with Robson, a press conference was called.

"I'm not happy," Brock, seated next to Robson, stated to the media. "In my opinion, the situation hasn't changed. Everything is the same in the contract. We have gone over just about everything you can think of."

"But I knew staying down in Alabama wouldn't do me any good. I knew I had to come back eventually, to work this thing out."

"Robson told us that if Dieter came back, he would work something out," said Scott. "So Dieter and I decided that we would take that first step and hope something would happen. I asked Robson if we could get something in writing and he had agreed."

"I told Dieter, as long as he was here playing there, to go into Robson's office every week and ask him about the progress of his contract."

Cal Murphy immediately placed Brock on a 14 day trial. "We will play him when he is ready," Murphy told the media. "If he isn't ready to play, we won't force the issue. We aren't going to forsake everything we have done up to the present just to get Dieter into the game."

"I don't think it's a matter of getting him into shape," he continued. "I think it's a matter of how quickly he learns and adapts to the system."

Paul Robson was a bit more optimistic. "You can do some simple addition," he stated. "You add the finest quarterback in the CFL to an already fine team and it comes out to some pretty positive things."

"I didn't get back to Winnipeg until the day before the first regular-season game," said Brock. "I did stay in shape with my workouts while I was in Birmingham, so physically I felt great. But I had missed the entire training camp. I didn't know the offensive system and I hadn't met many of the new guys yet."

"The first game was the next day in Winnipeg against Ottawa, but I didn't dress for it. I was staying at the Viscount Gort near the Stadium so I walked over and stood on the sidelines trying to be inconspicuous."

"I had met John Fourcade earlier that day. He was a quarterback that the Bombers had acquired from the B.C. Lions just prior to me coming back, so I was with him on the sidelines," said Brock. Fourcade had been the most valuable player of the 1982 Senior Bowl after passing for 115 yards and running for 33 yards and two touchdowns.

"I saw a few of the guys and they welcomed me back," said Brock. "But I didn't spend a whole lot of time because they were fixin to play."

Mark Jackson, who started against the Ottawa Rough Riders, struggled, managing just two points before being replaced by Nick Hall in the second quarter. Hall was impressive, running the Blue Bombers' offence, but he fell short as well. The Blue Bombers lost their opening game, 26-25.

"The next day, after the Ottawa game, was when I really got back with the team," said Brock. "From what I can remember, I think everyone was pretty happy that I was back. There may have been some who were still mad at me, but I didn't hear anything negative from anybody. It was business as usual."

"I had to meet all the new coaches and started learning the new offensive system. I still think that maybe the entire team, players and coaches were wondering if I was going to put everything into it. But one thing I can honestly say is that when I was playing or practicing, I always gave it everything I had."

"We were playing the Eskimos the next week so I spent a lot of time trying to learn Cal's new offensive system. I was in good shape and my arm felt great. The one thing I've always been proud of was the fact that I worked hard in the offseason and I was always in great shape."

Publically, Cal Murphy would not commit to naming his starter for the upcoming game, but John Fourcade had been released when Brock returned and Mark Jackson was placed on re-callable waivers.

"James Murphy had been there a few games from the year before and Jeff Boyd was a new wide receiver," said Brock. "Both of these guys were great receivers, but I had to get used to how they ran their routes. I knew it was going to be great once we got used to each other."

"When we got to Edmonton, I was rooming with Joe Poplawski so he could help me with the terminology," said Brock.

Nine minutes into the game, Murphy sent Brock in and he led the team to a dramatic come from behind victory. "Nicky Hall started the game, but he struggled early in the first quarter and that's when Cal put me in."

"I was still struggling a little bit with the terminology of the play calling, but a lot of those plays were similar to Ray Jauch's system," said Brock. "Joe Pop told me to just call plays from last year's system so I did and we were off and running. I think I threw a 75-yard touchdown pass to James Murphy and we ended up beating Edmonton 20-18."

"So, now everyone's happy and I'm fixin to start my first home game in Winnipeg against Hamilton the next week," he said. "I spent the entire time in practice getting comfortable with the new system. And yes, I did ask Paul Robson a few times if he had done anything with my contract. He said he was working on it."

The day before the home opener against Hamilton, Mark Jackson was released from the team. The 28 year old quarterback, who eight months earlier had been told that he had to fulfill his contractual obligation to the team, was now told to leave. He had been forced to decline several lucrative offers in the off-season and was now left to ponder his future.

"I expected to be booed as soon as I stepped on field," said Brock. "And they did. But after I threw a 40 yard pass to James Murphy, the booing stopped."

Brock finished the game with 21 completions on 49 attempts for 421 yards. His 49 pass attempts were the most in history at the time and were Brock's third best in his nine seasons with the team.

"More importantly, we won the game 29-18. That's the only thing that really mattered. And now everyone saw that I was going to play the best I could to help us win."

"The next week we had to go to Montreal and several of us went out for a few beers the night before the game. We came back to the hotel after curfew and Cal caught us. Everyone was worried the next day that if we don't win that game somebody was going to be sent home. I wasn't worried because of all we had gone through; I didn't think Cal was going to send me home."

"I remember it was very hot and humid in Montreal, but we are having a pretty dang good day," Brock recalled. "And we beat them, 30-25. I had another good game of over 400 yards passing. Everybody was playing great and we were winning."

"Then we went into Toronto the next week and beat them, 32-16. So that was four in a row."

With their record of 4-1, the Blue Bombers sat alone in first place in the Western Division. Winnipeg's Brock, Edmonton's Warren Moon and Hamilton's Tom Clements, were the top quarterbacks in the league after the first four weeks.

"My percentage was not real good, but that was going to get better with more playing time and understanding the offence better," said Brock. "But we were making a lot of big plays and I was throwing for an average of close to 350 yards per game."

"Now all I wanted was for Paul Robson to tell me he was doing something, anything about what we talked about back in Birmingham."

But unfortunately when Brock once again asked, there was nothing.

"All I wanted was some indication of something happening," said Brock. "That he would try to do something to come to some compromise so that I could just focus on playing the season. But there was always nothing; not a thing, not even a "we are looking into it" or anything. Whenever I went to see him, he wasn't available. I left messages that he wouldn't even return."

On his last attempt, Brock, clearly upset at the lack of movement, stormed out of the Blue Bombers' office right into a group of waiting reporters. "There is a problem," he told them. "I'm getting physically upset. It is really drawing on my mind and I want it solved."

"I came back to Winnipeg because I was hoping we could work something out. I held up my end of the bargain. Paul said if I came back, we would talk. I hate to say it, but I felt like I had been lied to."

At some point, Brock had even offered to buy out his own contract.

All this transpired on the same day the Blue Bombers had brought in another rookie quarterback, Scott Rutz for workouts.

Brock returned the next day for practice and took the offence through their regular sessions.

In B.C. Place the following week, the Lions embarrassed the Blue Bombers with a 44-6 win. Winnipeg fumbled the opening kickoff and 31 seconds later, The Lions' ran it for a touchdown, setting the stage for the entire game. Brock threw five interceptions and completed just 12 of 26 passes for 136 yards.

With the B.C. loss, the Blue Bombers were now tied with their next opponent, the Calgary Stampeders at 4-2.

Both teams started off slow, but Brock stepped it up using all eight of his receivers to complete 18 of 30 for 272 yards. Willard Reeves ran for two touchdowns on 14 and 13 yard plays to lead the Bombers on to a 36-21 victory.

Brock's touchdown passes in the victory gave him a career total of 187 and moving him into second place on the league's all-time list.

"When we got back to Winnipeg, I went back into Paul's office and again asked if he had done anything with my contract," Brock said. "He told me no, so I said that if I didn't hear something soon he should get somebody else ready to play."

"I wanted to stay with this team. That's the honest truth," said Brock. "I loved the guys on this team. But it seemed like the only way now to get anything from the Bombers was to hold out. So I walked away again and missed the afternoon practice. And I hated that."

Few people were ever aware of what transpired next. Cal Murphy wanted to have a private chat with Brock away from the Stadium. At Murphy's request, Brock drove a few blocks to Winnipeg's Westview Park. Murphy had ridden his bike and was waiting for him when he arrived. Westview Park is one of few elevated spots in Winnipeg where one can get a clear view of the entire city. The two men sat for several hours and talked.

"Cal said he didn't care about any of the stuff that was going on around me. He just wanted me to play football for the Bombers and him. He said he didn't care what I did, just show up and play to the best of my ability. I was already playing really well and he knew it. I think he also knew just how good we were as a team and just how far we could go."

"People always assumed that he and I didn't get along," he said. "But I loved that man."

On Friday, September 2, Paul Robson called a press conference and announced that Dieter Brock had been fined $10,000, one week's salary for missing practice.

"This football club is prepared to play the 1983 season, or another season without Dieter Brock. Through his irresponsible behavior to our football team, he has violated both the letter and spirit of his contract."

Chapter Fifteen

The thirty-three year old quarterback had had enough, and when faced with reporters outside the Blue Bombers' office, he didn't hold back. "If the Bombers don't want to resolve it, then they can trade me. Maybe some other club can resolve it."

While Brock sat inside his Westwood area home in Winnipeg, Winnipeg Blue Bombers GM, Paul Robson filed the necessary papers with the league's head office to have the quarterback suspended.

Within 24 hours of receiving the Blue Bombers' request, CFL Commissioner Jake Gaudaur approved the quarterback's suspension. Robson had thought the request would take up to 14 days as was the standard, but the league acted swiftly.

Speculation is that the league had been worried about losing some of their marquee players to the USFL and NFL which would result in dropped attendance and television rating. The Dieter Brock situation was a way of setting an example to other players that may be considering trying to leave.

"I didn't leave the house," said Brock. "The press went on the attack again and I didn't want to be recognized. People started driving by my house and screaming some pretty nasty things at us."

"It started to become a real circus. News crews were camped out in front of the house with cameras pointed in the windows trying to catch something. I decided to send my wife and daughters home to Birmingham. It wasn't fair to them to have them go through all that."

Marty York from the Globe & Mail published an article stating that Brock had told him he hated Winnipeg. It was York's piece where the now infamous phrase 'How many times can go to the zoo?' originated. The comment spread across news wires quickly and of course, was picked up by the Winnipeg media and repeated in various forms over and over. The comment even became the Globe & Mail's quote of the month in the Toronto newsroom.

"It was ridiculous," said Brock. "I don't remember exactly what I said, but we weren't really talking about the city of Winnipeg at all. It was taken way out of context."

"Back then, we didn't really know anyone in Winnipeg other than teammates and their families and they were all busy with the team. My family was only in Winnipeg three months of the year so there wasn't much time or opportunity to make friends. While I waited for something to happen, there was nothing for my wife and kids to do. They went to the zoo and the park a few times, but I didn't because I didn't want them subjected to the circus that was going on. They were bored, so they went home to get ready for the school year and where we had family and friends to be with. That's it. It wasn't meant as a shot on Winnipeg. But, unfortunately, I didn't get the chance to tell my side."

In 2006, Marty York was in Winnipeg to cover the Grey Cup game against B.C. Lions and the Montreal Alouettes. He used the quote again in another piece posted online by the Metro. But this time, he took the liberty of adding another degrading remark about the city.

> *"Years ago, when he was trying to get himself traded by the Blue Bombers, star quarterback Dieter Brock called me to deride the city of Winnipeg.*
>
> *"It's so boring," he said. "And it's so ridiculously flat. And, once you go to the park and the zoo here, there's nothing else to do. And, Marty, please make sure you quote me as saying all this in the paper."*
>
> *I did, sure enough. And Dieter was, sure enough, traded.*

And Winnipeg, sure enough, still is flat —
although that's not exactly what comes to your
mind when you see the waitresses at Earl's. I
mean, wow!

"I can tell you, anything that was said during that time was all just bullshit. It just became some stupid feud between me and the Bombers. Things were said that I don't believe either of us really meant."

"I certainly didn't hold anything against the city of Winnipeg for all this shit that was happening between me and the Bombers. I waited in Winnipeg for another week to see if anything was going to happen and that's when I decided that I needed to get the hell out of there and went home to Birmingham."

Without Brock, the Winnipeg Blue Bombers went on to lose to the Saskatchewan Roughriders, 32-30 and then experienced another loss to the Montreal Concordes, 30-18.

Trevor Kennard, the Blue Bombers' kicker, had sent Brock a seven page letter. "Him and I grew close," said Kennard. "He was my holder so after practices, we would go off and practice kicking when everyone else was gone."

"I remember Trevor's letter," said Brock. "He told me how much the team wanted me back."

But he wouldn't stay in Birmingham long before he and Gil Scott quietly arrived in Hamilton to meet with Harold Ballard, the Hamilton Tiger-Cats owner, and other executives from the team.

Fifteen hours later, Dieter Brock was one half of a blockbuster CFL trade. Hamilton had agreed to give up their all-star quarterback, Tom Clements for Brock, finally ending his relationship with the Blue Bombers. After nine and half years wearing the Blue and Gold, Dieter Brock he would now be wearing black and gold.

"After leaving Winnipeg I went back to Birmingham for four weeks before the trade to Hamilton was finalized. So, now I'm going to be in Hamilton by myself for the final six games of the season," said Brock. "And all I could think about during that whole time was just how great that team in Winnipeg could have been that year. Even though I had been with Winnipeg only six games I was getting more and more comfortable with the offence and I was thinking, did I do the right thing?"

"I'd gotten my contract shortened, but I was leaving a possible championship team. I know I'd forced all that to happen, but deep down, I wanted to finish my career in Winnipeg with a championship. Now that was all gone and now the only thing I could do was to play the final six games of this season and finish my CFL career in Hamilton."

Brock had accepted a one year deal with an option for the following year with the Hamilton Tiger-Cats. Harold Ballard admitted at a news conference that it was a deal he had been working on for quite a while.

"Harold Ballard loved Dieter Brock," said Gil Scott. "It was easy. Ballard wanted a deal, Robson didn't. It was that simple."

There was also speculation and unconfirmed reports that Paul Robson had been trying to put together a trade deal with other CFL teams involving Brock right from the beginning, but his asking price had been far too steep.

As luck would have it, Hamilton's head coach at the time of the trade was Bud Riley, the same man who had discovered Brock at the 1975 Senior Bowl in Alabama and was extremely aware of his value.

"We started thinking about the possibility of getting Dieter back in training camp," Riley stated to the media. "He'll be ready. He's run this kind of offence. He'll pick it up real quick."

"I had always liked Bud and it was good to be going to a team where I already knew the head coach well," said Brock. "But it really was strange to be going to a different team after being with the Bombers for all those years." Brock was joining former Blue Bombers' running back Mark Bragagnolo, linebacker Leo Ezerins and kicker, Bernie Ruoff.

On the other side of the trade, thirty-year-old Tom Clements was in his eighth CFL season. He had won the Schenley Award as the CFL's top rookie in 1975 with the Ottawa Rough Riders where he remained until being traded to Saskatchewan in 1979. During that same year, he was traded to Hamilton, but moved on to spend the 1980 season with the Kansas City Chiefs of the NFL. He returned to Hamilton in 1981.

Now, buoyed by the addition of a new veteran quarterback, the Blue Bombers hoped to take another step towards securing the top spot in the Western Division when Saskatchewan made another visit to the city.

The slumping Tiger-Cats were second in the Eastern Division at 4-6, two points ahead of the Ottawa Rough Riders, who they faced in their next game.

In their weekend debuts, Clements came out on top beating the Saskatchewan Roughriders 50-19, while Brock and the Ticats were 29-25 losers against Ottawa.

Hamilton led the game, 22-10 at halftime. Brock had run for one touchdown and passed for another to Ron Johnson. He had completed just 19-45 after only four days of working out with his new team.

In Winnipeg, back-up quarterback Nicky Hall would start for the Blue Bombers against the Roughriders because of his knowledge of Cal Murphy's offensive system. He took the Blue Bombers to a 10-7 lead mid-way through the second quarter. With 6:16 remaining, Tom Clements stepped onto the field. In his first series, he established control of the game, displaying his scrambling ability and talent for throwing the ball and led the Blue Bombers to a lopsided 50-19 victory.

"We've got some sanity here for a change," Murphy was quoted as saying after the game. "Now the players can concentrate on football."

Just two weeks after the trade, Dieter Brock and his new team played host to the Blue Bombers in what was being billed as a Brock/Clements match-up. The Blue Bombers would get their first look at Brock from the other side of the scrimmage line.

But five sacks in the game held Brock and his new offence to just 246 yards and a 34-19 loss. Blue Bombers' linebackers Tyrone Jones and Vernon Pahl were relentless in the pursuit of their former quarterback.

"When you're rushing against a drop back passer, it's heaven," said Pahl after the game.

Unfortunately, the Blue Bombers new found hope they had in their new quarterback wouldn't last. Tom Clements went down on the final play of the first half of the game with a fractured collarbone, forcing back-up, Nicky Hall to step in to lead. The early diagnosis on Clements was that he would be out for five to six weeks and there was just four weeks left in the regular season.

Two days later, the Blue Bombers would announce another trade. Quarterback Nicky Hall, receiver Nate Johnson, defensive lineman Jason Riley and an undisclosed 1984 draft pick were dealt to the Saskatchewan Roughriders for their veteran quarterback, John Hufnagel and rookie defensive end, J.C. Pelusi.

Cal Murphy had wanted an experienced quarterback on his team and he got one.

Seven days after the loss to the Winnipeg Blue Bombers, Hamilton head coach Bud Riley was relieved of his duties with the team. The firing didn't come as a big surprise to many because the Tiger-Cats had lost eight of their last twelve games, as well as some of their fan support.

"It's obvious we've been sliding downhill," Hamilton's general manger, Joe Zuger had told the media. "We felt a change was necessary to try, hopefully to save the season."

Riley had been in trouble since the Tiger-Cats lost two lopsided games; a 50-21 loss to Edmonton and a 50-16 loss to Toronto in September.

Now it was up to Al Bruno to salvage the 1983 season for the Hamilton Tiger-Cats.

Bruno had been drafted by the Philadelphia Eagles from the University of Kentucky in the third round of the 1951 NFL Draft, but chose to play for the Toronto Argonauts instead. He played two seasons for the Argonauts, one game for the Ottawa Rough Riders, and two seasons with the Winnipeg Blue Bombers.

His coaching career began in 1958 as a player-coach for the London Lords. After his playing career ended, he returned to Pennsylvania to teach and coach football at his alma mater, West Chester High School.

In 1966, Bruno returned to Canada as an assistant coach with the Ottawa Rough Riders. He left the Riders in 1968 and joined the coaching staff of the Hamilton Tiger-Cats. When head coach Joe Restic left to become head coach at Harvard, Bruno went with him to be the offensive coordinator.

Finally, after eleven seasons at Harvard, Bruno returned to the Hamilton Tiger-Cats as the team's Director of Player Personnel.

"When Al Bruno took over as the head coach, I really couldn't believe it at first," said Brock. "It seemed like Al just came out of nowhere. I was thinking what the hell is going on here because Al talked kind of funny and was kind of old school. I think he had played for Bear Bryant at Kentucky when the Bear was the head coach there."

"But as time went on, the more I got to know him the more I liked him," Brock continued. "Al was a true player's coach. He was the kind of coach that would listen to his players, especially the veterans. He did a wonderful job in Hamilton."

Brock and Bruno would face the Saskatchewan Roughriders in their first game together. Brock would combine with Tiger-Cats' receiver, Keith Baker for three touchdown passes and Hamilton's first win in four games. He was forced out of the game in the third quarter with a sprained ankle after completing 24 of 34 passes for 227 yards.

When leading the Blue Bombers, Brock was usually able to come out on top against the B.C. Lions, but when he changed uniforms, it wasn't the same. On October 22 in Vancouver, the Lions turned seven Hamilton turnovers into a 41-16 win.

Brock and his offence had just five first downs compared to twenty-five for the Lions. He fumbled twice, leading to two B.C. touchdowns and was eventually replaced with back-up Jeff Tedford.

Brock had always been was a dropback passer, but Hamilton's offensive line had been built to accommodate Tom Clements' scrambling ability.

Against the Calgary Stampeders the following week, Brock again had little protection from the line and was on the receiving end of four sacks in the 35-12 loss. He managed just one touchdown pass to slotback Rocky DiPietro for a four yard scoring play in the first quarter.

With one regular season game remaining in a 5-10 season, the Tiger-Cats were still in contention for a spot in the Eastern Division playoffs. Hamilton and Montreal had identical records and were set for a showdown at Olympic Stadium. Hamilton had won an earlier game 35-30, but Montreal had played better during the last month and the Tiger-Cats had struggled since Brock arrived. The Concordes had to win the game by more than five points in order to grab the last playoff spot in the East.

Before a crowd of 41,157, Brock connected early with Rocky DiPietro on a second and 20 from the Hamilton 38 yard line. One play later, he hit Scott Collie with a 14 yard pass before running backs Johnny Shepherd and former Bomber Mark Bragagnolo with runs of one and five yards, set the stage for a Bernie Ruoff field goal.

Montreal tried a last minute comeback, but Concordes quarterback, Kevin Starkey was intercepted on a long bomb attempt to end the game.

"We had to tie or win the last game of the season to qualify for the playoffs that year," said Brock. "We had a third down and 18 yards to go with just a little under a minute left in the game and we converted it. Bernie Ruoff kicking a field goal that tied the game 21-21 and we qualified for the playoffs."

On November 13, the Tiger-Cats faced the 8-8 Ottawa Rough Riders in the Eastern Division semi-finals.

Ottawa jumped to a 15-2 lead late in the second quarter. But Hamilton's offensive line, after heavy criticism all year, gave Brock the time he needed to win and advance the team into the finals against Toronto.

"I was finally getting back in rhythm after all the stuff that have gone on that year and started playing really well in the playoffs," said Brock. "Against Ottawa, I completed 28 out of 43 for 352 yards and we beat them 33 - 31."

In the West, once again the Blue Bombers road to the Grey Cup had to go through Edmonton, but 1983 was not to be the Eskimos' year. The Blue Bombers, with Tom Clements back leading the offence, beat the former Grey Cup Champion Eskimos 49-22.

The Toronto Argonauts had not beaten Dieter Brock for more than three years, but were ready try on November 20. Toronto head coach, Bob O'Bilovich admitted that his team had concerns about facing Brock once again, but felt his defence would be able to rise to the occasion.

"I know he's not going to hang on to the football," O'Bilovich had stated prior to the game. "He'll throw it away if he doesn't see a receiver. Or he'll eat it and take his losses. I knew it would take Brock some time to get used to his new teammates after he left Winnipeg. It wasn't going to happen overnight."

"The thing about the Toronto game was that I had been in the hospital for back spasms two days before the game," said Brock. "I had just gotten out the night before the game. I remember Jeff Tedford doing everything he possibly could to help me loosen up my back so that I would be able to play against the Argonauts."

The Argonauts were forced to play catch up right from the start after Brock and running back Johnny Shepherd combined on a 41 yard scoring play on their first offensive series. It was the first of three touchdowns for Shepherd in the game.

Hamilton led 15-1 at the end of the first quarter, 23-16 at the half, and 33-23 going into the third quarter. But Toronto would come back with 18 points in the fourth quarter and win the Eastern Division title, 41-36.

"We came within a horrible pass interference call from going to the Grey Cup in that Eastern final," said Brock. "We were up 36-34 with less than a minute to go when the official threw a flag on one of our defensive backs. It was a horrible call that wasn't even close to being pass interference. Toronto went on to score with 28 seconds left in the game and they won."

"I had been through a horrible penalty call against John Helton in the 1982 Western final and now this one that kept us from going to the Grey Cup."

"And in the Toronto game, I threw for almost 350 yards completing 23 out of 35 passes and two touchdowns, just coming out of the hospital."

In the West, a sellout crowd at BC Place of 59,409 watched as their Lion's beat the Blue Bombers 39-21. But losing the game wasn't all the Blue Bombers lost. For the second time in the season and third of his career, quarterback Tom Clements left the game with a broken shoulder. The 1983 season was over for the Winnipeg Blue Bombers as well.

"I felt pretty good about what happened at the end of the season in Hamilton," recalls Brock. "I knew I had one year left in the CFL, but I was determined to make 1984 a good year."

"I really liked playing for Al Bruno and there were a lot of good guys in Hamilton. I became really good friends with Jeff Tedford and on top of that, the quarterback at Jacksonville State, Ed Lett, was signed by the Tiger-Cats for the '84 season. Him and I became good friends as well."

"I thought '84 was going to be a fun year in Hamilton. I knew I had to move on from what happened in Winnipeg, even though I still wished that I could have finished my CFL career with the Blue Bombers."

"Still to this day, I feel like we could have won it all in that 1983 season in Winnipeg if things could have been worked out."

Chapter Sixteen

In early February 1984, the Winnipeg Football Club released their yearly financial report at a press conference. Club president, George Graham announced a net loss for the club's 1983 season of $536,000. The club had lost $756,000 on its football operations due to a drop in attendance.

General manager Paul Robson blamed the club's financial woes on the turmoil surrounding the Dieter Brock situation and the pirating of television signals by satellite dishes.

And once again, rumours of Brock's reluctance to report to Hamilton's training camp started making the rounds. It was reported that he was preparing to join the Washington Federals.

"That's just crazy," said Brock. "I was home in Birmingham. I knew this was going to be my last year in the CFL and I was determined to help my team win in any way possible."

Brock was so determined to make 1984 a winning year that he had started recruiting his own back-up late in the '83 season. It was his idea to bring in Ed Lett, a quarterback who broken all of Brock's records at Jacksonville State. As an all-star in the Gulf South Conference, Lett had also played with the Carolina Storm, a semi pro team in the American Football Association.

"Bringing in Lett was Brock's idea," said Hamilton general manager, Joe Zuger in a newspaper interview. "Dieter told us about this 25-year old quarterback, who had broken all his records at Jacksonville State. We figured we'd give him a chance, but until he's in a few scrimmages and maybe an exhibition game, we won't know how he'll work out."

In their first pre-season game, the Tiger-Cats beat the Argonauts, 13-6. Brock played the first and last quarter going 7-17 for 95 yards. By the end of the pre-season, Hamilton would be 2-2.

In the first regular season game which took place in Montreal, Brock took the Ticats to a 25-0 first quarter lead on two touchdown passes. Following that, he quickly turned a blocked Montreal punt into another touchdown. He went 18-20 for in the first half and finished the game with 310 yards on 20 completions with 30 attempts. Hamilton's total offence for the game was 446 yards and a 49-31 win. There was no doubt that Brock still remained one of the premier quarterbacks in the league, proving his worth by shredding a stunned Montreal defence.

On July 8, the Saskatchewan Roughriders made a trip east to face him and the Ticats. Hamilton's running back Kelvin Lindsay ran for two touchdowns while Brock scrambled for a third in a rare 27-27 tie. Brock went 47 of 58 with 415 yards with just two interceptions. He had engineered late drives that saw the Tiger-Cats score fourteen points in the final 1:19 of the game.

But in game three of the season, the Ottawa Rough Riders jumped to a 28-0 lead in the third quarter, eventually winning, 31-9. Rough Rider quarterback J.C. Watts threw three touchdown passes in a game that Brock could only go 18 of 33 for 201 yards.

The back spasms that had bothered him late in the previous season started to flare up again, forcing Brock to miss the next game. Back-up Peter Gales stepped in, but without offensive weapons like fullback Mark Bragagnolo, running back Johnny Shepherd and receiver Ron Johnson, who were also out with injuries, the Ticats went down in defeat against the Calgary Stampeders, 23-18.

Brock returned to the roster just in time to face his former team, the Blue Bombers, but would have to compete without Bragagnolo in the backfield again. The Winnipeg defence held him to just 21 of 38 for 191 yards and forced an embarrassing 42-20 defeat.

"Going in, I knew how good they were on offence and their defence had been getting better and better over the last couple of years," said Brock. "But honestly, it was just another game to me."

After a two week bye, Hamilton would host their Eastern Division rivals, the Toronto Argonauts on August 12. The Argonauts dominated much of the game and it was only in the fourth quarter when Brock and the Tiger-Cats were able to get their offence moving.

Brock was able to connect on 34 of 50 passes for 382 yards. He hit Rocky DiPietro and Ron Johnson for touchdowns, but it wasn't enough of an effort. Argo quarterback, Condredge Holloway and kicker, Hank Ilesic lead the Argos to the 30-22 win.

On that same evening in 1984, 2000 miles south of Hamilton, former Edmonton Eskimos quarterback, Warren Moon, who had been let out of his previous CFL contract, was making his home field debut with the Houston Oilers of the NFL. Moon would lead his team to a 36-17 pre-season victory against the New York Jets in just his second consecutive start in the league.

The following week, against the visiting B.C. Lions, Brock threw two interceptions, fumbled once and was sacked four times in a losing effort of 19-11.

The Tiger-Cats were now on a five game losing streak and Brock had only thrown two touchdown passes during the team's decline.

"There's no way we can win if I give the ball away," Brock was reported to have said after the game. "We had opportunities, but didn't capitalize on them. My mistakes killed us and I've got to improve."

Once again, Brock was starting to feel that all too familiar heat from fans and the press. He was being blamed for his lack of ability to find key receivers in the open. He seemed to be struggling with the game plan and wasn't getting the extra effort from his teammates.

"Al Bruno had hired Elijah Pitts as the offensive coordinator that season," recalls Brock. "Eli was an ex Green Bay Packer running back in their championship years with Vince Lombardi and Bart Starr. He had been coaching in the NFL for several years and I think he was just out there looking for another job when the Hamilton position came open. He had decided to take it just to buy time before getting back into the NFL."

"But Eli was a great guy. I really liked him a lot. He was fun to be around and really understood the game. Jeff Tedford and I were given the reins to run the offence. Eli had basically told us to go put the game plan together and he let us run the offensive meetings."

"I remember Eli telling me he couldn't believe I'd been in the CFL for this long. He told me I had the best arm he had ever seen and he couldn't believe that I hadn't gone to the NFL yet," recalls Brock.

"Throughout my entire CFL career there had been a number of players released from NFL teams that had come into Winnipeg and Hamilton. They told me they couldn't believe how well I threw the ball."

"I would hear it all the time," he said. "It started to bother me a bit. No one in U.S. knew who I was or what I had done."

In Edmonton the following week, Brock was picked off twice in the fourth quarter by the Eskimos' defence. The first interception led to Eskimos quarterback Matt Dunigan hitting his receiver for a 26 yard touchdown just six plays later. Then, within minutes, Edmonton's Darryl Hall's grabbed a Brock interception which led to a Dave Cutler field goal.

In total, the Edmonton defence intercepted four passes, recovered one fumble and sacked Brock five times. The final score was Edmonton 35, Hamilton 14.

With his team now sitting with a 1-8-1 record for the season, Head Coach Al Bruno was frustrated. He was quoted in the press after the game, saying, "Too many guys just weren't ready to play."

"We really were a good team," said Brock. "But we weren't consistent. We couldn't seem to finish a game strong. We had the talent, but just kept making mental mistakes and we weren't able to execute the game plan that we wanted."

The Tiger-Cats, with their backs against the wall, proved they were good team by ending their seven game winless streak on September 3 with a 30-11 win against the Montreal Concordes. In that game, Brock passed for two touchdowns, one of them to Rocky DiPietro which became a club record, 365 receptions.

The following week, the B.C. Lions, fresh off a two week break, dominated the Tiger-Cats. In the 46-11 B.C. win, Brock was sacked seven times and eventually replaced in the fourth quarter by back-up Jeff Tedford.

On September 15, Dieter Brock would return to Winnipeg to face the 8-2 Blue Bombers with his 2-7-1 Tiger-Cats. This was his first trip back to the city since his hold-out and the big trade between him and Clements. When the league released the 1984 schedule, he had noticed the date and tried to not let it bother him. His plan was to treat it like any other game on the schedule.

In most leagues, the Hamilton Tiger-Cats should have been far out of the play-off picture. But being in the Eastern Division, there was still a glimmer of hope for the team. But the Blue Bombers were going to be a challenge.

As the game moved on, the teams were tied 10-10 at half-time. But in the end, it wasn't even close with the hero of the game being Blue Bombers' receiver, Joe Poplawski. That evening, Poplawski moved past Ernie Pitts to become the Winnipeg Blue Bombers' all-time leading receiver and his team went on the beat the Tiger-Cats, 48-16.

The Blue Bombers sacked their former quarterback five times and caused one interception. But even with the Bombers' relentless defensive pursuit, Brock still managed to complete 20 of 35 passes for 248 yards. In the second half, he watched helplessly as his former team exploded for 38 points.

The win put the Blue Bombers in sole possession of first place in the Western Division, extending their home game unbeaten streak to five games.

Unfortunately, Brock's performance and Joe Poplawski's milestone reception were over shadowed by the constant chorus of Brock-Busting fans who booed the Hamilton quarterback throughout the entire game.

Ten days after the game, columnist, Jack Matheson once again chose Dieter Brock as the subject of his syndicated MCNA column, but this time, there was a difference in the context of his piece.

Usually, I'm proud of Manitobans in general and Winnipeggers in particular. They're tough, because they have to be to endure January and February. They're buddy-buddy, they have big hearts if you give them the right sob story, they've got more couth than you'll find in Upper Canada or B.C.

They're good people – most of the time. I don't mind saying they lost me on the night of September 15th, and I wanted to crawl in a hole before any unsuspecting tourists found out I live here. The whole province was getting ready for a visit by the holiest of fathers the next day, and so on that night a whole bunch of rabble made us look like scum on national TV.

It was the return of Dieter Brock that did it. The man who didn't like it here came back "home" with his new football team, the Hamilton Tiger-Cats, and the fans who don't believe in live and let live really put on a show. They hooted and hollered derisively every time Brock stepped on the field, and it was sickening.

So he didn't like it here, all of a sudden, where is it chiselled on a concrete sidewalk that everybody has to live in Winnipeg and worship at the shrine of Bill Norrie? So he said that after you've been to the zoo there's nowhere else to go, what's wrong with that? As far as I know, we still have free speech in this country.

Okay, so have some fun, like the guys and girls who went to some expense to dress up like bears and apes and things, a not-very-subtle reminder about Brock's trip to the zoo. Hang some banners, keeping them in good taste. Let Brock know you remember, but after five minutes put a plug in it. Unfortunately, too many alleged football fans got

*carried away the other night. Suddenly, Brock
wasn't the crock, the Winnipeg crowd was.*

*How soon they forget. They came prepared to
crucify Brock for wanting to change scenery, which
is every man's inalienable right, I would think.
They chose to forget what he had done for
Winnipeg in nine other years.*

*He threw more passes for Winnipeg and completed
more than anyone except Ronnie Lancaster, who
played for 19 years, or more than half of his life. He
completed 57 per cent of his passes, which was
more than Lanky did. He completed 195 passes for
touchdowns, more than Sam Etcheverry, Russ
Jackson, Warren Moon, Tom Clements, Tom
Wilkinson, Joe Kapp – well to make a long story
short, everybody but Lancaster, again.*

*In the seven full seasons he was leader of the band
here, Brock won 65 games and lost 47. Perhaps the
yahoos would have preferred Benji Dial.*

*Dieter Brock left a lot of blood on the grass at the
Winnipeg ball park, and so Winnipeg said thank
you by shrieking, cursing and razzing it as loud as
possible. Not for five minutes for the whole game,
and there oughta be a law. To his credit, Brock
blocked it out and played a helluva game, and it's
just too bad he doesn't play for a helluva team. He's
suffering enough, being associated with those
humpty-dumpties, without being dumped on by
people who used to be his friends.*

*I can hear the rebuttal now. Never mind the
statistics, he never won the big game, never got us
to the Grey Cup game. Right on, and if that makes
him a loser, so is John Bonk, he's been here longer
than Brock was and he's never been there either.
John Helton never won a Grey Cup, does that make
him a social outcast? Lancaster played 19 years
and won one Grey Cup.*

*It's all relative. And as far as Winnipeg football
fans are concerned, on the night Dieter Brock came
back to town, they should have been ashamed of*

themselves. It wouldn't have happened anywhere
else in Canada, and I'm willing to bet.

The following week, after shaking off the Winnipeg experience, Dieter Brock got his offence moving after Ticats defensive back, Felix Wright picked off Stampeders quarterback, Greg Vavra. Wright ran the ball in for a touchdown and Brock also ran for a touchdown in a winning effort of 29-26 against the Calgary team.

Their next game turned into a 28-21 loss to the Eskimos, but it became a turning point in the season for the Hamilton team. With a record of 3-9-1, head coach, Al Bruno summoned his team to a meeting in the Regina hotel before their game against the Roughriders

"He gave us a little speech and explained the situation to us," Brock was quoted as saying. "Basically, he told us to start playing or get the hell out."

After an inconsistent, slow start to the season, Brock and the Tiger-Cats took Bruno's words to heart and started a late season surge by defeating Saskatchewan, 31-8, Ottawa, 20-14 and Toronto, 25-20.

Those three regular season victories left them with a 6-9-1 season record and in second place in the Eastern Division behind the Toronto Argonauts and ahead of the Montreal Concordes.

On November 4, in the Eastern Division semi-final, they beat third place Montreal, 17-11 and were set to face the Argonauts in Toronto the following week.

Ticats' kicker, Bernie Ruoff would be the difference maker in the tight overtime 14-13 win. His record setting 56-yard field goal in overtime secured Hamilton's place in the 1984 Grey Cup.

Labeled as underdogs from the beginning of the season, the Hamilton Tiger-Cats, with Dieter Brock as their quarterback had advanced to the Grey Cup final in Edmonton against hia former team, the Winnipeg Blue Bombers.

In an article by Jeff Blair from the Winnipeg Free Press, Ticat's safety and former Blue Bomber, Paul Bennet spoke about seeing an emotional Brock in the locker room following the Toronto victory.

"I thought back to when I knew him in Winnipeg and I could never remember him showing that much emotion," Bennett stated after seeing Brock in tears.

"But then I thought about it and I realized he's probably never been as much a part of a team feeling before. It was good to see. A lot of people seem to think he's playing out the string and that he doesn't care about things and just wants to get out of here and go to the U.S."

Bennett was a hard-hitting safety and a fierce punt returner who played with the Hamilton Tiger-Cats from 1984 to 1987 after being with the Winnipeg Blue Bombers from 1980 to 1983. Winnipeg had traded him to Toronto in early 1984 before he landed in Hamilton for the balance of the '84 season.

"In a way, I understand what he went through after the problems I had this year," Bennett stated in the article. "Your family really should be the most important thing in life. All he wanted was the best for them."

"We were all emotional after that game," Bennett said recently, recalling the event. "What Dieter went through, what I went through, what Leo Ezerins and Dan Huclack went through, honestly after all these years the memory has faded, but I will tell you, we were all emotional in what was an awesome win. And we loved Dieter. He was a great quarterback and we were thrilled that he was with us."

"His players loved him," said Bennett. "As a guy who played with him and against him, I respected that man. He scared the crap out of any defensive secondary because of his arm strength and his ability to throw deep. He was one of a kind, a great quarterback."

It was no surprise that in the days leading up to the big game, it would be billed as a battle of Brock versus Clements. 7,000 Blue Bomber fans assembled inside the Winnipeg Convention Centre five days before the game to give their team a send-off. But instead of cheers and well wishes, the evening's theme song "Brock Busters" dominated throughout the crowd.

In an interview just days before the game, Brock had stated, "The media might want to call it that, but I really don't look at this game as me against Tom Clements. What

I've got to worry about is what I do against the Winnipeg defence."

Going into the 1984 Grey Cup, almost all of the experts believed the game would be a complete mismatch, with the Winnipeg Blue Bombers heavily favoured. They turned out to be correct, but not before Brock and the Tiger-Cats stunned the Bombers by jumping out to an early lead.

For the first twenty minutes of the game, Hamilton built 14-0 and 17-3 leads. In one of their first offensive series, Brock was able to cut through the Blue Bombers' defence for a 15 yard touchdown run.

"When he was with us, we told him not to run the ball," recalls Blue Bomber centre, John Bonk." We used to call him Chicken Legs. We told him not to run for two reasons; he wasn't very good at it, and he looked stupid when he did."

"And what's the first thing he does in the game?" asked Bonk. "He runs it in on us and we're down seven points."

Blue Bombers' quarterback Tom Clements was ineffective in the opening 15 minutes, getting picked off twice by Hamilton's Felix Wright and Mark Streeter. Both interceptions led to Hamilton scores; the first was Brock's 15-yard run and the second was a seven-yard pass to Rocky DiPietro.

But the Blue Bombers would soon dominate and take over the game. Their initial points came on a 25-yard field goal by Trevor Kennerd to close out the opening quarter. In the second quarter, after Bernie Ruoff kicked a 20-yard field goal to give the Ticats a 17-3 lead, the Bombers responded with 27 points to close out the half.

Tom Clements, who played almost the entire game with a rib injury, improved as the game wore on, completing a 12-yard touchdown pass to Joe Poplawski to give Winnipeg the lead for good.

But the key turning point in the game came at 2:26 before halftime, when Brock was sacked hard by Blue Bombers' linebacker Tyrone Jones. The ball was jarred loose from his hands and nose tackle Stan Mikawos recovered the fumble and ran 22 yards for a touchdown. That put the Bombers in front 24-17.

Willard Reaves went on to score a pair of touchdowns for the Blue Bombers, both on three-yard carries. Despite being limited with an injured shoulder, Reeves still managed to run for 64 yards in the game. Winnipeg cornerback David Shaw intercepted a Brock pass in the second quarter, returning the ball 26 yards to the Hamilton 28 to help set up one of Reaves' TD runs.

Finally, Winnipeg's back-up quarterback, John Hufnagel, threw a four-yard touchdown pass to Jeff Boyd in the fourth quarter to complete the scoring and giving the Winnipeg Blue Bombers their first Grey Cup win since 1962.

"Certainly Tyrone Jones, their front seven and a really outstanding secondary were key for them in that game," said Brock. "They had a really solid defence in '84, one of the best they had in years."

"We really had no running attack at all," said Brock. "I think our leading rusher on the year had only 300 yards. And I think we were hurting at wide receiver. Rocky di Pietro was our only thousand yard receiver."

"It would have been a monumental task for us to win that game," he recalled. "It would have taken Winnipeg making a lot of mistakes and us capitalizing on those mistakes for us to even be in the ballgame. That's kind of what happened early in the game, where we had gotten a couple of interceptions and drove those opportunities down field for touchdowns."

"We played pretty good offensively early on, but after that the Bombers settled down and stopped making mistakes. We just couldn't continue the pace offensively and once they took control that was it for us."

The Blue Bombers had sacked Brock five times in the game which seemed to delight the 68,000 spectators who joined in singing the "Brock-Busters" theme song throughout the first half.

Winnipeg had 483 yards of net offence compared to the 205 yards for Hamilton. Tom Clements and back-up, John Hufnagle combined for 23 completions on 32 passes for 311 yards. Brock on the other hand, hit 21 of 42 for 198 yards.

Blue Bombers' quarterback, Tom Clements was named the offensive player of the game and Tyrone Jones, who had four of the five sacks on Brock, was named the top defensive player.

"I have to admit, here I was playing my last game in the CFL and it's in the Grey Cup against the team that I wanted to end my CFL career with," said Brock. "Even though I enjoyed my last year in Hamilton, it was tough not to think of what might have been if I had stayed in Winnipeg and I still think about that. It's still difficult today."

The 1984 Grey Cup was the last time Dieter Brock took to the field in a Canadian Football League uniform. In his ten seasons in the CFL, Brock had complied 34,830 yards on 4,535 pass attempts and 2,602 completions. He threw 210 touchdown passes and had a 57% completion ratio. As a Winnipeg Blue Bomber, Dieter Brock was the CFL passing leader in 1978, 1980, 1981 and 1984. He was awarded All-Western Quarterback in 1980 and 1982, All-Canadian Quarterback in 1980 and 1981, the Jeff Nicklin Memorial Trophy in 1980 and 1981. He also received the Schenley Award for Most Outstanding Player in 1980 and 1981.

On November 30, 1984, the Winnipeg Free Press published one of their last mentions on Dieter Brock. It was just a three lines claiming that he had left the city of Winnipeg without paying a $35 fine for an outstanding parking ticket.

Chapter Seventeen

On March 1, 1985, Dieter Brock would become a 34year old free agent when his contract with the Hamilton Tiger-Cats expired. Ticats' owner Harold Ballard had offered him $500,000 per season to stay with the team for another two years, but Brock had made his intentions clear from the beginning; it was time to go home and play football.

His decision was far more personal than the "fame and fortune," label members of the media had repeatedly pushed out. "It was something I felt I had to do," said Brock. "It had nothing to do with money or disliking anything about Canada or Winnipeg or Hamilton. If I didn't at least try to make it, I would have regretted that for the rest of my life."

Because no NFL team had drafted him out of Jacksonville State, Brock was free to make the best deal he could. But one of the issues facing him was that no one really knew who Dieter Brock was or what he had accomplished in his eleven years in the CFL.

More than two dozen major newspapers in the U.S., including his own hometown Birmingham newspaper claimed Brock had led the Winnipeg Jets to a Grey Cup title.

Brock now jokes at the situation. "Hell, I don't think Birmingham ever got that right"

But at the time, it wasn't really a laughing matter. In an environment where young boy dreams of seeking glory in the National Football League, anything less can be a disappointment.

By the end of Brock's eleven seasons in the Canadian Football League, he had thrown for 34,830 yards, which would place him third among NFL quarterbacks behind Fran Tarkenton and John Unitas. Everyone knew those names. Brock was twice named the C.F.L.'s most valuable player, but in his home country, no one even knew what a Shenley Award was.

In an interview with the Santa Ana Orange County Register, Brock's long-time friend, Snapper Lancaster said, "I thought about that when Joe Namath got into the Hall of Fame. He's a real favorite around here and that's great for him. But Joe passed for 27,000 yards and here Diete's got nearly 35,000 in his 11 years.

In eleven years, his parents had only been to Winnipeg a couple of times to see their boy play, while his brother, Wild Bill, once inseparable, had never seen him perform on Canadian turf.

And now, twelve years after playing in the Senior Bowl in Mobile, Alabama, the 34 year old unknown quarterback was going to have to make an impression and hope someone "back home" would appreciate his talent and capabilities.

By mid-January, just eight weeks after the 1984 Grey Cup loss, Gill Scott notified every NFL team by letter that his client was available and eager to play south of the border. Seven teams showed an interest in him and three; the Green Bay Packers, the Philadelphia Eagles and the Buffalo Bills agreed to fly him in for a workout.

The first stop on the Dieter Brock Tour was Buffalo where the Bills offensive coordinator was said to have been an admirer of Brock.

"We know, number one, that he's a very good competitor," said Bills coach Kay Stephenson. "He seems to get the ball in the end zone. He seems to come out a winner."

One week later, after seeing Brock work out, Stephenson had said, "Our interest in Brock is very great and we probably are going to be talking with him and his people relatively soon." Buffalo had finished the '84 season with a record of 2-14, the worst in the league. They had been waiting on Jim Kelly, who was with the USFL's Houston Gamblers were growing impatient.

The Green Bay Packers were also getting close to making a decision. Packers' head coach, Forrest Gregg, had been familiar with Brock from the one year he spent coaching the Toronto Argonauts in 1979.

But Gregg couldn't promise the one thing Brock was seeking, a starting job. The Packers' had Lynn Dicky, who had led their offence to a then-team record of 429 points in the 83 season. His 4,458 yards that season had also served as a team record.

As word continued to spread around the league, the Cleveland Browns and Los Angeles Rams stepped up and started to inquire about the quarterback.

John Robinson, the head coach of the Rams had told the L.A. Times that his team was interested in acquiring another quarterback. He had seen Dieter Brock on film and agreed that he was a good player

Don Seeholzer from the Santa Ana Orange County Register wrote that Robinson had also said, "I think we've looked at him like a lot of clubs. We're one of about twelve teams that probably looked at him. Our interest isn't any different than any of the other twelve teams might be."

On the negative side, almost every team had their concerns. In question was Brock's ability to adapt to the National Football League with its narrow field and one less player on each side. And the issue of his age also kept creeping up.

But Robinson, from what little he knew of the quarterback, had said he thought Brock could come in the NFL and play the following year. "He wouldn't embarrass himself. I have a tendency to think that. I don't think a guy like that can come in and say nobody has a chance."

It was becoming common knowledge around the league that Gil Scott was seeking a four-year contract for his client, but he disputed the rumoured $500,000 a year salary, stating it was too low.

In an interview, Scott had said, "I believe Dieter is worth a salary commensurate with the top quarterbacks in the NFL. Not a million a year, but among the top."

In 1984, the five highest paid quarterbacks in the NFL were Houston's Warren Moon at $1 million, Denver's John

Elway at $900,000, San Francisco's Joe Montana at $858,333, Green Bay's Lynn Dicky at $850,000 and San Diego's Dan Fouts at $750,000.

Back in Winnipeg, a few sportswriters who still questioned Brock's value south of the border, wrote that he would be lucky to get a back-up position and his salary wouldn't come close to $300,000.

But Brock was determined to be an immediate starter or at least have an opportunity to challenge for a starting job in the NFL.

On March 23, the Buffalo Bills made the quarterback an offer of $1.8 million over four years. The amount of $400,000 per season was almost double what Brock had earned in his last year with the Hamilton Tiger-Cats.

Green Bay stepped up with a similar financial offer a few days later. But money wasn't the issue for Brock, it never was. He had stated he would go where he felt had a chance of a starting job and there was no way he would receive that in Green Bay as long as Lynn Dickey remained active on the roster.

Then, the Los Angeles Rams called and wanted to see more. On Monday, March 25, Dieter Brock stood in Rams Park in Anaheim, California with head coach John Robinson and a handful of other team executives. Two members of the media were invited to attend the display.

Before the workout, the members of the media had described Brock as more like the lead singer in a rock group rather than a quarterback. They stated he looked five years younger than his actual age.

But after the brief twenty minute workout, they labeled him as the strongest new arm in town.

"I was very impressed," admitted Robinson after the work out. "He has an outstanding arm. This only reinforced what I believed before the workout. He is a good player who will be a success in the National Football League."

"I've coached a lot of great quarterbacks in my day, including Dan Fouts when he was at Oregon," Robinson had told a bystander according to Sports Illustrated. "This guy may be the best I've ever seen throwing the ball."

What followed was an unexpected, swift signing. Robinson went to lunch with several team executives and the club's legal counsel and by late afternoon that same day, the Los Angeles Rams had a new starting quarterback. Brock signed a four year agreement worth $2.1 million.

There was no question about the strength of his arm, but some had concerns over his age. Thirty-four was relatively old for an NFL player, but not necessarily for quarterbacks. Going into the 1985 season, thirteen teams had intended to start quarterbacks who were 30 years or older, and eight of them were Brock's age or older.

At the press conference announcing his signing, Jack Faulkner, the Los Angeles Rams' administrator of football relations had said, "Because he has taken care of himself so well, staying fit, he's like 34 going on 25. People are always screaming about getting a young player in. But sometimes, you have to take an older guy to get you through a season or two before you can find a younger guy."

He then grabbed Brock's arm and joked to the media, "They're Popeye arms."

"As a quarterback," said Brock at the same press conference. "I didn't want to go to a situation that was rebuilding. I don't have the time. This team has a legitimate shot at getting to a Super Bowl. I wanted to be a part of it."

But the L.A. agreement did not guarantee a starting job and that didn't seem to concern him. "I just feel this is an excellent opportunity for me and I'm not afraid of competition," he had said. "This is a dream come true. To me and my family, this was the best place to live, plus coming to a team with personnel like the Rams."

While no guarantees were made, Robinson left little question as to who would likely open the 1985 season. Vince Ferragamo had signed a four year contract extension with the Rams in the '84 season. "We've talked to Vince and told him we would seek an opportunity to trade him where he will have every chance to succeed. I think that's probably the right thing for both of us."

In 1984, Ferragamo started as the Rams' quarterback. But in a 24–14 loss at Pittsburgh in Week 3, Ferragamo broke his right hand and had not returned to the lineup for the remainder of the season.

In 1981, Nelson Skalbania, the then new owner of the Montreal Alouettes, had signed Ferragamo to a one year $600,000 contract. It was the same year the Winnipeg Blue Bombers had balked at paying $200,000 for Dieter Brock.

"After I signed and everything was finalized, I went back to Birmingham for a few weeks to get some things together," said Brock. "We went back to L.A. for a week or two to find a house to buy. We found one in Villa Park, an area that was about fifteen minutes from Ram Park where our facilities were. Ram Park was probably three or four blocks from the amusement park, Knott's Berry Farm. Disneyland was just down the road as well."

The Brock's had moved twenty-three times in eleven years and were excited to finally settle into their new home in California.

"And then it was time to get to work," said Brock. "I went back to Anaheim and spent about two months learning the system and working out with the guys."

Certain players had been participating in off-season drills. Brock worked out with the other quarterbacks and receivers. He had been competing with 1984 back-up Jeff Kemp and newcomer Steve Dills, but he had gone from a virtual unknown to a clear frontrunner for the Rams starting position in just a few short weeks.

"I went to back to Birmingham about six weeks before training camp was to begin to get things together for our move to our new house in Villa Park. I was playing a pickup basketball game with the guys when I felt my back give out. I sat down for a while hoping it would go away. It wasn't the first time that had happened. I had a few incidents back in Canada, but it usually went away after a few days."

"But it didn't. I showed up to training camp without saying anything," he recalled. "I wanted to just work through it."

But on July 18, he was forced to miss practice because of what was officially reported as a slight soreness in his lower back. The team decided that he would be held out for the rest of the week.

His absence was hardly noticed because the L.A. Rams had another issue that had been playing out with the team. As usual, what would a professional football training camp be without at least one player holdout?

Eric Dickerson, the Los Angeles Ram's running back who had run for 2105 yards in the '84 season and broke O.J. Simpson's single season NFL rushing record, refused to report to training camp because he claimed the team had reneged on a verbal agreement for a contract extension.

Dickerson was in the third of a series of four-one year contracts totaling $2.2 million. "Right now the Rams can end the contract whenever they want," Dickerson had claimed at a press conference. "If I get hurt, get paralyzed or break a leg and can't play football again, the Rams aren't going to take care of me for the rest of my life. Who's going to take care of me, of my mother, pay for my mother's house? Who's going to meet those notes every month?"

Dickerson, a star at Southern Methodist and the NFL's No 2 draft pick in 1983, had signed a four year, $2.2 million contract with the Rams before his rookie season. He had received half of the financial portion in cash in the beginning, including a $600,000 signing bonus, a $300,000 bonus for reporting to camp and a $150,000 first year salary.

In addition, Rams' owner Georgia Frontiere gave Dickerson a $40,000 Porsche and paid to redecorate his condominium. She had also installed satellite TV at Dickerson's mother's home in Texas so she could watch all the Rams games.

"I was so concerned with learning a new offensive system and what I had to do as a quarterback that Eric's situation wasn't something that I worried about at all," said Brock. "We already had Heisman Trophy winner, Charles White, a smaller running back who was probably in my opinion, one of the toughest players I've ever played with."

"I'm not even sure if I even met Dickerson before he showed up for that season," Brock said. "I don't remember him being there during the early workouts when I was out there. And when he did come back, I really didn't get to know him too well, or anybody else for that matter."

"Compared to the Blue Bombers or even the Tiger-Cats, this seemed like more of a job. We would come in early in the morning and the quarterbacks and receivers would usually watch film together or we would have quarterback meetings and then break for lunch before heading out to practice."

On August 10, Dieter Brock made his NFL debut. The L.A. Rams, with Brock starting, faced Warren Moon and the Houston Oilers. While most of the pregame hype had centered on the Ram's 34 year old rookie, the most effective quarterback that evening was his old CFL rival, Warren Moon.

Moon completed 8 of 15 passes for 105 yards with one interception in the two quarters he played. Brock was 5 of 12 for just 49 yards in his limited time on the field, but the Rams came out on top with a score of 7-3.

Coach Robinson had said after the game that he thought Brock had done a good job. And for the most part, Brock was relieved to have his first game behind him.

With the press hovering around his locker looking for a statement, he told them, "Well, it wasn't a blazing offensive show, but the key thing was I felt confident and I felt I knew what I was doing out there. That's a plus."

In his second pre-season game, Brock completed 10 of 19 passes for 145 yards and put the Rams ahead of the St Louis Cardinals 20-0 at halftime. The final score was 39-7 and the Rams' pre-season record was 2-0.

"I thought Dieter Brock had a perfect game at quarterback," Coach Robinson had said after the game. "He looked like he had played in the NFL for 11 or 12 years."

Ram's running back, Barry Redden, who had stepped in for the missing Dickerson said in a postgame interview, "I knew from day one when I saw him that he had an arm. I think he can lead us to a Super Bowl."

The next pre-season game came close to being a Canadian homecoming for Brock. Initially, the L.A. Rams had been scheduled to play the August 24 exhibition game against the Philadelphia Eagles in Toronto, but it seemed the threat of competition had angered some CFL executives.

"We are vehemently opposed to what we consider an invasion of our territory," CFL commissioner Doug Mitchel had said in a Canadian press story. Mitchell had indicated that NFL commissioner Pete Rozelle had called as a courtesy just to get Mitchell's opinion on the game and he certainly received it.

After their conversation, the game was quietly moved to Ohio Stadium in Columbus, Ohio.

Brock turned in his shakiest performance of the early season in the game. Not only did the Ram's offence fail to score, their deepest penetration ended at the Eagles 45 yard line.

"We never really got anything going," said Brock after the 14-12 loss in which he threw his first NFL interception. "No excuses. We didn't play well. This wasn't my first bad game and won't be my last."

In their final pre-season game, Brock threw a 21 yard touchdown pass to Henry Ellard and running back, Barry Redden scored on a 3 yard run to beat the New England Patriots, 14-13.

"He knows the game," said Robinson after the game. "He has good instincts, understands when to throw the ball and what the defence is doing. And his attitude has been great."

But what impressed his new team the most, was Brock's work ethic. "I've seen lots of guys hit the weights," said Robinson. "But no one like this guy. Some of our players are afraid to even approach him in the weight room. That's how intense he is in there."

On September 8, 1984, as the oldest rookie in league history, Dieter Brock was finally presented with the opportunity to live out the dream that he had carried for so many years; he was the starting quarterback on a National Football League team.

And it was well worth the wait because when the final whistle had blown that evening, Dieter Brock and the Los

Angeles Rams had beaten John Elway and the Denver Broncos, 20-16. Dieter Brock was 1-0 in the NFL.

The statistic sheet recorded that he was 16 of 29 passes for 174 yards, but that wasn't the true story of the game.

With two minutes left in the game, down 16-13, Brock engineered an almost perfect 80 yard drive. He went 5 of 5 for 68 yards and capped it off with the winning touchdown. Steven Spielberg couldn't have scripted it it any better.

Brock threw less than what he was used in the Canadian Football League, but when asked by the press if beating the Denver Broncos was more fun than beating the Ottawa Rough Riders, he replied with a smile, "Damn right it was."

"I tried to take it as just another game, but I knew it was not just another game."

"The question you ask about a quarterback is, 'Can he play when things are not going right?'" said coach John Robinson after the game. "These are the things that make a successful quarterback. And he's going to be a successful quarterback."

In Week Two at Veterans Stadium in Philadelphia, the Eagles decided to start their 22 year old rookie Randal Cunningham instead of veteran Ron Jaworski. For the Rams, Eric Dickerson had arrived but would watch from the sidelines while Charlie White ran a club record 36 times for 144 yards. It wasn't much of a passing game in the early stages and like the week before, Brock put together a stunning fourth quarter winning drive. The nine play, 84 yard series finished with a Charlie White 17 yard touchdown run. The Rams beat the Eagles 17-6.

After two games, Dieter Brock was rated twelfth in the league and was set to take the 2-0 Rams into Seattle against the 2-0 Seahawks.

Week Three saw Eric Dickerson, in his first game of the season, carry the ball 31 times for 150 yards and three touchdowns as the Rams beat the Seahawks 35-24. Brock went 12 of 24 passes for 203 yards.

Brock would have the biggest day of his four game NFL career the following week against the Atlanta Falcons. He completed 16 of 20 passes for 25 yards, defeating the Falcons 17-6.

On a play that had been designed to merely produce a first down, Brock threw 64 yards to receiver, Henry Ellard for the touchdown.

In Week Five, the Rams beat the Minnesota Vikings 13-10 to remain unbeaten at 5-0. Brock went 14 of 20 for just 144 yards in a game that saw the Ram's defence dominate the game.

Week Six was the second consecutive week that the Rams' defence proved to be the difference in the game by intercepting four passes, two for touchdowns in the Rams 31-27 victory against the Tampa Bay Buccaneers.

Overall, the Los Angeles Rams ranked fourth defensively, second against the rush and eighth against the pass. Dieter Brock was ranked seventeenth among quarterbacks in the league with 75.5 rating points.

"Yes, we were 6-0," said Brock. "But I I knew I had to keep improving. My back still wasn't great. I was throwing much less than I ever did in the CFL and that took some time to get used to. The biggest adjustment was that I had been used to calling my own plays, but that was different now, too. Coach would send plays into the huddle. That takes longer and it hard to get a good read of the defence because you're rushed."

Despite their unbeaten record, it seemed the L.A. Rams and especially, Brock were still not getting the respect they deserved around the league. Being one point underdogs to the upcoming 3-3 Kansas City Chiefs, it was obvious the Rams and their quarterback had yet to make believers out of everyone, but it certainly hadn't been for their lack of trying.

At his weekly media breakfast, coach Robinson had stated, "I think there was a genuine prejudice against Dieter coming into this league. I'm appalled when I hear people say Dieter can't read defences."

Robinson then provided numbers showing that over the previous three weeks, Brock had been the league's highest rated quarterback, superior to the likes of San Francisco's Joe Montana and Miami's Dan Marino.

Riled up and ready to prove the world wrong, the Rams went into Kansas City and shut them out, 16-0. Eric Dickerson ran for a touchdown and Mike Lansford kicked three field goals. The Rams' defence intercepted Chief's quarterback Todd Blackledge six times in the lopsided game.

But in that game, Brock was only able to connect on 9 of 20 passes for just 68 yards and some could tell that something was not right.

"It started the night before the game," Brock recalled. "I started getting sharp pains in my side. They had given me medication for that night, but it didn't help and they weren't sure exactly what it was."

"When we got back to L.A., I made a doctor's appointment and it was diagnosed as a kidney stone."

"We played the San Francisco 49ers the next week at home," said Brock. "That would be our first loss of the season after seven consecutive wins."

The Rams had fallen 28-14 to Joe Montana and the 49ers, but Brock, in pain, had made history by throwing more passes in that game than any other Rams' quarterback. He went 35 of 51 passes for 344 yards with three interceptions.

That evening, he had no choice. The kidney stone had dangerously flared up again and the pain was unbearable. Brock check himself into Chapman General Hospital in Orange County after the game. He was released the next morning with orders to rest and drink fluids, hoping the stone would pass naturally before the team's next practice.

But whether the stone passed or not, Brock and the coaching staff were adamant that there was no chance he would miss the next game against the New Orleans Saints in five days.

Coach Robinson, known for his sarcasm, stated to the media. "When I was in med school, I was absent the week we worked on kidney stones. I don't know. We're just gonna have to wait and see."

"We were playing the Saints at home," said Brock. "My brother and a few friends from Birmingham were coming out to watch the game. I was pretty excited."

By Thursday, Brock was back on the practice field preparing for the Saints game. He had told team officials that he was not in any pain, and hid the fact that he was. It had been decided that if the stone had not passed by the following Monday, it would have to be surgically removed.

Against the 3-5 Saints, midway through the second quarter, Brock began an 81 yard drive by completing a 19 yard pass to receiver Bobby Duckworth. Four plays later, he passed 35 yards to Tony Hunter, moving the ball to the Saints 16 yard line.

Brock then completed the drive by throwing a 17 yard touchdown pass to Henry Ellard, giving the Rams a 14-0 lead.

With Wild Bill Brock and friends in the stands cheering on their hometown hero, the Rams went on to beat the New Orleans Saints 28-10. But what should have been an evening of celebration, instead turned into a cause for concern for many.

"Bill had an epileptic seizure during that game," said Brock. "And I was taken to the hospital because the kidney stone flared up again. It had gotten really bad."

"I think maybe Bill had some bruises from the seizure, but he seemed to be okay afterwards. But I had to stay in the hospital."

"I had to have the kidney stone operation the next day which meant I was going to miss the next game in New Jersey against the New York Giants."

The doctors removed the stone through an incision in his lower abdomen after an unsuccessful attempt to do so arthroscopically. The stone had impacted in his ureter and had become a threat to his kidney, which necessitated the surgery according to media reports released from his doctors. He was required to remain in the hospital for two to three days.

Without him leading the offence, the Rams fell 24-19 in the Week Ten match-up with the New York Giants.

"I came back thirteen days later and we played the Atlanta Falcons in Atlanta, "said Brock. "But I was pissing blood before and after the game. I had to play with the stent they put in. It was supposed to have been taken out, but they decided to leave it until after the next game."

The Atlanta Falcons, a team with two victories in their last 20 games handed the Rams their third loss in four games by a score of 30-14. The Rams managed just 157 yards of total offence, 45 of those were rushing. Two early fumbles by Ron Brown and Charlie White put the Rams behind 10-0 and the team just couldn't come back.

Against the Green Bay Packers in Week Eleven, the Rams' Ron Brown returned two kickoffs for touchdowns, including the opening kickoff which he returned 98 yards. The second was 86 yards and he also caught a Brock 39 yard pass for a third touchdown. Brock was near perfect completing 15 of 19 passes for 150 yards.

The Packers did counter with two touchdowns and a field goal to take a temporary lead in the third quarter, but Dickerson would put the Rams in front on a 14 yard run, leading the team to a 34-17 victory.

"We beat the Packers which was one of the teams that wanted to sign me after I left the CFL," said Brock. "After that game I went back into the hospital and had the stent removed."

On December 1, the New Orleans Saints would get their revenge for the earlier blowout by sacking Brock nine times and recovering 3 fumbles. Saints' kicker Morten Anderson kicked five field goals in a 29-3 victory.

For the first time in his NFL career, Brock was pulled from a game. Back-up Jeff Kemp was sent in with 12 minutes left in the game. In his least productive outing of the season, Brock had completed just 5 of 10 passes for 49 yards with one interception and seven sacks.

"I know I was on the receiving end of some very hard hitting defensive plays," he said to the press after the game. "And it's not easy playing a game with your butt pasted to the ground."

In Week 14 in San Francisco, the 49ers looked to be in control until Rams' receiver Henry Ellard scored on a tipped pass from Brock and cornerback Gary Green returned an interception for the winning points. Brock went 16 of 22 passes for 160 and a touchdown in the 27-20 victory.

After taking heat from the media for the previous losses, Brock was uncharacteristically emotional after the win. "It was exciting just from the fact of the crap I've been hearing all week and stuff," he said during the interview. "Things like I couldn't quarterback a college team and that stuff. I think that was in a San Francisco paper."

In Week 15, against the St Louis Cardinals, Brock had one of his best performances as a Rams' quarterback as the Los Angeles team clinched their first NFC West Division crown since 1979. He passed for four touchdowns, while Dickerson ran for 124 yards and two touchdowns. The Rams rolled up 425 yards of offence in the 46-14 victory.

Having clinched a playoff spot with an 11-4 record, the Week 16 game against the Los Angeles Raiders wasn't much of a factor for the team, but it was for Brock. A clause in his contract stipulated a $25,000 performance bonus if he was able to finish the season as either the number one or two quarterback in the league. Going into the game, he was ranked second just behind the 49ers, Joe Montana.

But in a lackluster performance at home on a Monday night, the Rams could only muster two field goals and Brock was sacked six times with just 14 of 28 passes for 159 yards in the 16-6 defeat.

In his first NFL season, Dieter Brock finished third with a pass competition percentage of 59.7 per cent, missing his $25,000 performance bonus by two competitions. He finished eighth in passer rating with an 82 and was sacked 51 times. He completed 218 of 365 passes for 2658 yards and 16 touchdowns.

It was an impressive performance, but he was still being blamed by the Los Angeles fans and media for the Rams' unimaginative offence and their last place ranking in passing yardage.

"At times I wonder what I've got to do," he said in an interview before their conference semi-final against the Dallas Cowboys. "Sometimes I ask myself what Dan Fouts or Dan Marino's stats would be if they threw the ball 22 times a game. We're ranked last in passing because we've thrown the fewest amount of passes. But I can't complain, we're where we want to be."

In the conference semi-final, the Dallas Cowboys did not look like the 10–6 team that had won their division title. The Cowboys were blown out at home in Texas Stadium by the Rams 20–0. Eric Dickerson set an NFL playoff record by rushing for 248 yards including touchdown runs of 55 and 40 yards. He outgained Dallas' entire team and was responsible for 78 per cent of the Rams 316 yards of total offence.

Brock completed just 6 of 22 passes for 50 yards. He completed 1 of 9 second half passes for minus four yards. But despite his performance, the win put the Los Angeles Rams in the NFC Championship Game against the Chicago Bears.

The Chicago Bears defence had dominated every game in the '85 season and their performance in the NFC Championship would be no different.

Bear's head coach Mike Ditka said in a pre-game interview, "Brock is small. And we plan on making him even smaller."

The Bears' defence held Eric Dickerson to just 46 yards in rushing, forcing him to fumble twice. They held Brock to 10 completions out of 31 attempts for just 66 passing yards. While the Bears offensive numbers were hardly impressive with just 232 yards, Los Angeles gained just 130 yards of total offence in the game.

After forcing the Rams to go three-and-out on the game's first possession, Bears' quarterback Jim McMahon threw two consecutive 20-yard completions to tight end Emery Moorehead and receiver Willie Gault before finishing the drive with a 16-yard touchdown run on third down and 10.

Bears' kicker Kevin Butler added a 34-yard field goal to give Chicago a 10-0 first quarter lead. With 1:04 left in the second quarter, L.A. had an opportunity to get back in the game when Dale Hatcher's punt bounced into the leg of Bears defensive back Reggie Phillips and safety Jerry Gray recovered the ball for the Rams on Chicago's 21-yard line. Dickerson rushed twice for nine yards and caught a pass for 7 yards, but on his reception he was tackled on the 5 yard line just as time expired in the half.

On the first drive of the second half, Brock drove the Rams to their own 47-yard line, but Bears' linebacker Otis Wilson forced a fumble from Dickerson that was recovered by defensive back Mike Richardson on the Bears 48 yard line.

Faced with fourth down and 6 on the Rams 35-yard line on the ensuing drive, Chicago picked up a first down with McMahon's 13-yard completion to running back Walter Payton. The Bears' would then take a 17-0 lead on McMahon's 22-yard touchdown pass to Gault on the next play.

Brock would then respond with a drive into Chicago territory, but Leslie Frazier would end it with an interception.

With 2:37 left in the fourth quarter, Dent forced Brock to fumble again while sacking him and linebacker Wilber Marshall picked up the loose ball and returned it 52 yards for a touchdown.

The Bears' defensive front snuffed any hopes the Rams' offence might have had about controlling the game. For the 41st time in the last 42 games the Bears had possession of the ball longer than their opponent. Brock, who was mauled from the opening play never seemed to get on track.

His longest completion of the day was a 15-yard pass to Tony Hunter in the fourth quarter. His best throw was up the right sideline to rookie Michael Young, but was ruled incomplete because Young had stepped out of bounds. Video replays later showed that cornerback Mike Richardson had pushed Young after the legal bump zone, but no penalty was called.

Michael Young went on to play 10 years in the NFL. After leaving the Rams, his best years were with John Elway and the Denver Broncos, and in 1991 he led the team in catches and receiving yardage. He still remains close to Elway and gives a stunning answer when asked whether Elway had the strongest arm of all the quarterbacks he caught.

"Nope, Dieter Brock with the Rams," Young said in a 2012 interview with the Orlando Sentinel. "The ball was still rising when it got to you."

The Los Angeles Rams would end their 1985 season with a 24-0 loss while the Chicago Bears went on to beat the New England Patriots, 46-10 in Super Bowl XX.

For the next few weeks, the Los Angeles media were so obsessed with blaming Brock and Coach Robinson, they seemed to forget that the Rams had finished 11-5 in the regular season, beat Tom Landry's Dallas Cowboys in the conference semi-finals and then, under adverse conditions at Soldier Field, played the Bears as competitively as any other team in the league.

But in sports, it's never, "What have you done?" it's always, "What can you do now?"

Chapter Eighteen

Shortly after his team's disappointing NFC Championship loss to the Bears, Dieter Brock made his way back to Canada. He was welcomed as the key note speaker in Toronto at a charity fundraiser benefiting the Easter Seals Foundation.

Reports claimed that the highlight of the evening came when Brock, standing at the podium said, "I know a lot of you people appreciate what I did up here, but I've been taking a lot of heat in L.A. I guess the only way to be a popular quarterback in the States is to look like one." He then, in Jim McMahon style, put on a pair of dark sunglasses and a head band which read 'Easter Seals.'

"I still haven't got my trophy," he joked.

Despite setting a Rams' team record for completion percentage during the '85 season and finishing in eighth place with a passer rating of 82.0, his performance was still being labeled as poor.

Everyone ignored the fact that the Los Angeles Rams' offence had originally been geared to the run after acquiring Eric Dickerson and the passing offence had not been a priority in the previous year. Prior to his signing, Robinson had told Brock and his agent, Gil Scott that he wanted to open up his offence, but that never transpired in 1985.

"We threw the ball the least amount of times in the league," Brock had said. "If we were supposed to get balance, you'd think we'd throw the ball a bit more."

"The press in L.A. we're just waiting for me to have a bad game so they could pounce," said Brock. "That's the way they do it. But the stats on those two playoff games don't tell the true story. Nobody seemed to want to say that there were six dropped balls in that Cowboys' game. I'm not talking about hard catches, I'm talking about easy catches and one of them should have been a touchdown. Yup, nobody wanted to say anything about that."

"It was widely reported that I completed just 6 of 22, but they never mentioned I had dislocated my finger right before halftime. Not that it affected anything in the second half, but nobody wanted to say anything about it."

"And nobody wanted to say anything about the bad calls in the Bear game, either. One was a 60-yard completion that would have put us at the 15-yard line with the first down going in. Another one that we should have had was a field goal attempt at the end of the first half, but the officials blew the whistle early."

"These aren't excuses, they're just facts. Facts that were never told."

"How can a quarterback who has a record of 11-4, with the third highest completion percentage in the NFL, and who was the eighth rated passer in the league, and in the last 12 games of the regular season had the highest passer rating in the NFL, with a completion percentage of almost 64 per cent be considered a bad quarterback? That is bullshit!"

In the off-season, Coach Robinson had started to see the light and added Dick Coury to the team's staff.

Coury, originally from Los Angeles, had been around the league for years and he knew football, specifically offensive schemes. His journey had taken him to Denver, Portland, Philadelphia, San Diego, Boston, New Orleans and to three pro football leagues.

In March 1986, he came home with an assignment from John Robinson as the Rams' quarterback coach.

In an interview with Tim Tuttle of the Santa Ana Orange County Register, Coury discussed his new role with the Los Angeles Rams.

What did you and Robinson discuss about the job? You're probably aware that Dieter Brock has taken a lot of criticism.

I think a lot of the criticism is based upon that bad game with the Bears. The Bears made a lot of quarterbacks look bad this year. All Coach Robinson wants me to do is coach the quarterback and make sure somebody is looking and working with the guy all the time. It frees him up to be more involved with the total offence. He doesn't want to have to zero in on the quarterback himself, but at the same time, he wants somebody to coach every move the quarterback makes. I think he is also counting on me to come up with some pass offensive thoughts that we've used before. Basically, my job is coaching the quarterback.

What are your early impressions of Brock?

I've looked at five films, the first five games of the season. To be perfectly honest with you, I was impressed with the way he drops back, he's got a strong arm, and he's tough and stands in there, gets rid of the ball at the last second. I think any time you come into the National Football League, no matter if you've been playing in Canada, in college or in another league, it is a real experience for you. I was completely shocked and amazed at how good the defensive people were, how fast they run and the athletic ability they have.

The back problem that bothered Brock through much of 1985 season continued nagging him. During the off-season, he had bought an orthopod and began hanging upside down from his thighs to stretch out his spine. It worked for a while, but the pain just kept returning. In desperation he started adding an intensive series of daily stretches and exercises and finally felt he was well enough to report to training camp with minimal discomfort.

On April 12, Coach John Robinson announced the Rams had come to terms with former Atlanta Falcons' quarterback, Steve Bartkowski. After a brief workout the following week, the Rams were impressed enough to offer Bartkowski a one year contract to join the team.

Robinson had stated that without a doubt the 33- year old former free agent was being brought in as a support player only and not as a replacement for Brock.

"Dieter will be No. 1," he told the press. "And he'll start out at quarterback and we'll go from there. I don't think the signing of Bartkowski means any change for him at all."

But Brock saw things differently. "If Bartkowski is better than me, he should be playing," he said in a telephone interview. He had yet to talk with Robinson and discuss the situation. "The best guy's got to play; that's the way it's got to be. What I don't want to happen is to be led along if they've already decided on Bartkowski."

"Jeff Kemp had been sent to the San Francisco 49ers to backup Joe Montana," said Brock. "He started in 1984 after Vince Ferragamo had been playing poorly, and was my backup in 1985."

"So, I was there in the 1986 off-season, working out just like I had done before the '85 season," recalls Brock. "The only difference for me that year was that we lived out there. I worked out at Rams Park four days a week with the other quarterbacks and receivers."

Coach Robinson opened the L.A. training camp on July 14, at Cal State Fullerton. Unfortunately, on the second day Brock was forced out to rest because his lower back pain had flared up again.

"His back's sore, so we're going to have to stop his activity," Robinson told the press during the daily press gathering. "I would put it in the category of a nagging injury at this point."

But privately, according to team trainer, Jim Anderson, Brock had a narrowing of the disc spaces in his lower back from a combination of age and the physical pounding he'd taken on the field throughout his career causing some pinching of the nerves. He was given shots in hopes of reducing the inflammation and to manage the pain.

On July 23, Brock admitted that his days in the sport could be numbered. "The back did bother me a lot last year and especially during the off-season," he said. "While I'm definitely concerned about it, I'm not ready to announce my retirement just yet. The injury isn't going to go away no matter what I do, but I think I'll be able to perform as expected this year."

A few days later, he was back participating with the other quarterbacks in seven on seven scrimmages against the San Diego Chargers. Steve Dills went 9 of 13 for 117 yards, Steve Bartkowski was 9 of 13 for 129 yards and Brock finished with 5 of 14 for 76 yards.

But the crowd in attendance made it clear who they wanted as their quarterback by booing Brock after two incompletions and cheered the arrival of Bartkowski.

The following day, John Hall of the Santa Ana Orange County Register published a piece that almost echoed the same sentiment as the 1984 Jack Matheson column in Winnipeg.

"The way the Anaheim Stadium spectators treated Brock at Thursdays nights' 7 on 7 passing drill and rookie scrimmage with San Diego was shocking even to an observer who has been shocked so often and so many times over the years that his hair would be standing on end like Don King's if only he had enough left to put in the electric socket.

They even booed Dieter's drops.

The main reason I feel so rotten about the Brock situation I guess, is that besides being unfair and unreasonable, I believe the sports writers have had so much to do with it.

Our criticism of his deficiencies last season got out of control. Criticism of a poor performance is one thing, complete cheap-shot ridicule for the mere sake of a good line, is quite another.

It simply became fashionable to sink a harpoon in Brock. We all share some balance, and we all should be ashamed.

What did this guy do? He may not be the best QB in the NFL, maybe not the best even on the Rams. But he isn't some sort of subhuman who steals from the blind and gives people cancer.

He didn't mess with drugs, he didn't beat his wife, he didn't send his three daughters to work in a sweatshop, and he didn't come home drunk and kick the dog.

All he did, without complaint, playing hurt when he had to, in sickness and in health, in his first season in the NFL was quarterback the Rams to an 11-5 division championship and all the way into the NFC title game with the Bears.

One writer in particular has turned into an absolute lunatic on the subject. You'd think Brock hasn't completed a pass in his life.

He completed 218 passes for 2,658 yards and had a completion percentage of 59.7 per cent in an offence not geared for big passing numbers.

As Mr. QB of Them All, Tarkenton, also once observed, 'Every quarterback has faults as any leader has faults. He is obviously very vulnerable because if he doesn't complete every pass and win every game, somebody will find something negative to say about him – the coach, the fans, the press, somebody. If he isn't super-confident, he'll become paranoid just wondering who will be shooting at him next.

The least we can do is put down our guns for five minutes and give Brock a chance."

In the Ram's first pre-season game on August 5 against the Oilers, the Rams trailed 7-0 in the first quarter. Brock, the designated starter, had moved the offence to the Oilers 6 yard line, but out of nowhere, Oiler's safety, Bo Eason took him down hard. Minutes later, Brock limped off the field, but was out for the game with what was originally reported as a bruised knee.

He was able to return to practice two days earlier than anyone had expected which didn't surprise Coach Robinson. "He's a tough guy. That's the reason he came back. He's a tough guy." When asked by the media.

Brock may have been a tough, but he certainly wasn't a lucky. On August 11, it was announced that he would have to undergo arthroscopic surgery to repair a partially torn medial meniscus cartilage in his left knee and was expected to miss 4 to 6 weeks.

"I hate to say better now than later, but at least I have a chance to get back for the rest of the season. I've just got to go on," Brock commented.

Steve Bartkowski was set to take over the starting position until a strained abdominal muscle sidelined him before the last pre-season game. Back-up Steve Dills would finish the pre-season.

By mid-September, the Rams acquired highly-touted rookie, Jim Everett from the Houston Oilers. They had signed the former Purdue quarterback to a $2.7 million four year contract.

"I think they are determined to get somebody in here who's got a chance to play for years in the future," Brock stated in an interview. "I've got to look at it as a positive move for the Rams."

"I was put on injury reserve and I had to miss the first four games of the regular season," said Brock. "I traveled with the team for the first few games, but didn't dress out because I couldn't play," he said.

"But I'm telling you, if I could have played, I would have. Had I been the starting quarterback during that 1986 season, there's no doubt in my mind that we would have done very, very well."

No sooner had Brock returned to his throwing exercises with the team when he aggravated his lower back again. The team physiotherapist once again gave him a set of strengthening and stretching exercises, hopping to return to practice in the following week. "I was rehabbing and actually started to do the on field workouts, but my back started bothering me."

"And then, back in Birmingham, my brother Bill had a seizure and hit his head," said Brock. "He passed away. I didn't know much about the details, but it hit me hard."

"I came back from the funeral and was sent to several doctors to get more back injections. When that didn't work, I was sent to more doctors to get their evaluations."

"I was finally diagnosed with degenerative disc disease in my lower back which is the wearing down of the discs that causes bone on bone pain," he said. "There's no cure except to stop playing was the advice from the doctor. If it was real severe, just to have a normal life, they could have done a fusion, but that's not recommended to play football."

In early December, Dieter returned to Birmingham to have his back looked at by a local neurosurgeon with hopes of finding an answer. But based on that recommendation, he would be undergoing back surgery in the near future.

Then, to add insult to injury, on Thursday, December 11, while still in Birmingham, he received a telephone call from the Rams informing him that he was being released. The club had agreed to make good on all contractual obligations including medical payments and playoff bonuses, but only if he failed to sign with another team.

In early January 1987, in desperation, Brock travelled to San Francisco to see Dr. Arthur White, the same back specialist that had operated on Joe Montana earlier that year.

Gil Scott reportedly stated in an interview, "Dieter definitely doesn't feel he's done with football yet. But he can't play in the state he's in right now. That much we know."

In late May of 1987, the Brocks sold their Villa Park home in Anaheim and moved back home to Birmingham, Alabama.

Two months later, Dieter Brock sat down with a reporter from the Birmingham News and informed them he had ruptured discs and a cracked vertebra in his lower back. His condition would definitely require major surgery if he hopped to ever be able step back on the football field again.

"To have something like that done would be crazy," he stated." I'd have a 50 percent chance of successful surgery and being able to come back to play, and 50 percent is just not good enough."

In 1986, the Los Angeles Rams, without Dieter Brock, began their season with three straight wins against the St. Louis Cardinals, San Francisco 49ers, and Indianapolis Colts. But by Week 4, the Philadelphia Eagles had upset the Rams, 34–20. They would win four of their next five, including a 20–17 win over the Bears in a rematch of the NFC Championship Game.

The Rams would then close out the season with losses in four of their final seven games to end the year with a record of 10–6, one loss more than Brock's 1985 season.

They finished the '86 season in second place in the NFC West behind the 49ers compared to first the previous year.

In the playoffs, the Rams lost to the Washington Redskins, 19–7 in the NFC Wild Card Game to end the season with an overall record of 10–7.

In 1987, the Rams struggled right out the gate. In their first two games against the Houston Oilers and Minnesota Vikings, the Rams had 4th quarter leads and blew them.

The next week, a strike occurred which wiped out all Week 3 games. One week later, the Rams were beaten by the Saints 37-10 to start the season 0-3.

They would finally get in the win column the next week, beating the Pittsburgh Steelers at home, 31-21. However, the next week in Atlanta, the Rams lost another big lead, this time after leading 17-0 at halftime and 20-7 in the 4th quarter.

This was followed by embarrassing losses to the Cleveland Browns, their archrival San Francisco 49ers, and the Saints to drop to 1-7, the team's worst start since 1965.

The season ended with the Rams getting pummeled by the 49ers on the road, 48-0. Ultimately, the Rams finished the strike-shortened season 6-9 and missed the playoffs for the first time since 1982.

In 1988, in what should have been Dieter Brock's last season, the team improved from a disappointing 6–9 record, to going 10–6, and qualifying as a Wild Card before losing to the Minnesota Vikings in the NFC Wild Card game.

On November 27, Dieter Brock watched from his home in Birmingham as Denver Bronco's John Elway passed for three touchdowns and run for another in a 35-24 victory over the Los Angeles Rams.

"I tried to get the Grey Cup game on that day, but we couldn't see it down here. I really wanted watch the Blue Bombers win that Grey Cup," he said quietly. "Better yet, I should have been there. Because all along, that was my team."

Epilogue

At some point, someone may write about the rest of Dieter Brock's life, because that last chapter is definitely not the end of his story.

There is a twelve year span of coaching and teaching with organizations such University of Alabama at Birmingham and the Alabama State University. There's also the early nineties when he returned to the Canadian Football League as an offensive coordinator for the Ottawa Rough Riders, Hamilton Tiger-Cats and the Edmonton Eskimos.

He was recognized and inducted into the Jacksonville State Hall of Fame and the Alabama Sports Hall of Fame.

In 1990, he was inducted into the Winnipeg Blue Bombers' Hall of Fame with Earl Lunsford, Bill Frank and Joe Poplawski. And in 1995, Dieter Brock took his rightful place in the Canadian Football Hall of Fame. In 2016, he was inducted into the Winnipeg Blue Bombers Ring of Honour with players like Jack Jacobs, Doug Brown, Leo Lewis, Milt Stegall, Ken Ploen and Chris Walby.

On his CFL Hall of Fame induction page it states;

After graduating from Jacksonville State in 1974, Dieter Brock signed a one-year contract with the Winnipeg Blue Bombers and assumed the starting quarterback role in October, 1975. Always known for his strong arm, Brock trained by throwing weighted steel balls at a target.

Brock had 34,830 yards on 4,535 pass attempts and 2,602 completions. He threw 210 touchdown passes and had a 57% completion ratio. On October 3, 1981 Brock completed 41 passes, 16 of

*them consecutively, and completed an outstanding
87% on the day. He was the CFL passing leader in
1978, 1980, 1981 and 1984.
Brock played in the 1984 Grey Cup championship
where his team lost to Winnipeg.*

Dieter Brock was inducted to the Winnipeg Football
Hall of Fame in 1990.

There's no argument that Dieter Brock was and still is a
famous quarterback for his achievements on the field. His
statistics are impressive and his records stood for years.
But it really doesn't matter how many Hall of Fame
inductions he received because none of them will ever tell
the true story of who Dieter Brock really is. And they
certainly don't recognize the sacrifices he made to get
there.

Throughout his career, Dieter Brock was faithful in the
little things that we never saw. Bud Riley, Ray Jauch and
Cal Murphy, three of the all-time greatest CFL coaches,
taught him how to lead with wisdom and humility, to
develop the perseverance and resilience he needed to see
his way through the challenges he faced on and off the
field. They helped him develop the patience he needed to
spot the openings in an opponent's defence and take
advantage of it. Those lessons are what developed his
wisdom of the game and allowed him to stand proud on the
podium and accept two Shenley Awards, not for himself,
but for the entire team.

His passion and dedication for the game was evident
even after he had retired. In early 1986, prior to the start of
the NFL season, New York Giants quarterback, Phil Simms
contacted Brock to get his advice on off-season training.
Brock willingly detailed his training regime to Simms who
had heard stories of the "greatest arm in football." Later
that same year, Simms was named Most Valuable Player of
Super Bowl XXI, after he led the Giants to a 39–20 victory
over the Denver Broncos. He also set a record that season
for the highest completion percentage in a Super Bowl at
88 percent, completing 22 of 25 passes.

In an early September 1985 interview with the Santa
Ana Orange County Register, Brock's long-time friend,

Snapper Lancaster revealed a side of Brock that few ever saw. "A couple of times he got so low up there in Canada," Lancaster had said of Brock, "And once he came home and said, 'I just can't take it anymore.' But through all that he just got better. Even when he got traded from Winnipeg to Hamilton, he said, 'I can't go up there and not be my best. I have to do the best I can.'"

"He was homesick. It was never about the money or fame," said Snapper. "Diete was just a kid who wanted to come home to throw the ball as far as could and to the best of his ability."

Let's face it; Dieter Brock didn't change the world. He didn't even win a championship with the Winnipeg Blue Bombers. What he accomplished on the field will someday be forgotten. His records will be broken and his statistics are going to fade over time. That's just the way it is in sports. But what will be remembered are the moments he gave us, both on and off the field.

There are all those dramatic fourth quarter comebacks where Joe Poplawski, Mike Holmes, Eugene Goodlow, Henry Ellard or James Murphy would stretch out to grab a game winning touchdown pass. We'll remember those side pitches to Eric Dickerson, Jay Washington or Willard Reeves at just the right moment that would break a game wide open and give us hope.

There were seasons where his ailing back should have kept him sidelined, but the game was far more important. There were games played with braces, medication and surgical stints.

Off the field, there was his offer to forgoing a large portion of his salary for the return of teammate Butch Norman when the Winnipeg Football Club was struggling financially. He provided transportation for another teammate, Frankie Smith, who had limited resources when he relocated to Winnipeg to play. He played two NFL games with a surgical stint in his abdomen and an entire season with a failing back to get his team to the playoffs. He paid off the mortgage on his parent's home, even after their relationship had been strained.

"It was never about him," recalls Gill Scott. "It was always about family, team and the game."

"In all my years of football, I've never seen anything like him," said Ray Jauch. "He was one of a kind."

The Brock Buster t-shirts and signs have been replaced by joy and excitement on the faces of fans today. They line up for hours to get an autograph or and just shake the hand of a legend. There's never a mention of holdouts or contract disputes and when the Zoo is brought up now, it's done so in jest and followed by a laugh from both parties.

Jason Johnson, the pastor at River City Church in Winnipeg recalls a story about Brock that never made headlines. "When I was a kid growing up in the Brandon area, I used to get bullied in elementary school," said Johnson. "My dad was signed with the Blue Bombers in the '70s, but never played with them. In order to gain favour with the bullies, I used to say that I 'knew' Dieter Brock, given my dad's Bombers' connection. When I did that, the fists stopped and they left me alone."

"Fast forward to 2016 when Dieter was inducted into the Ring of Fame at Investors' Group Stadium," he said. "I met him and told him that story. It was a moment that I didn't search out, it was just an opportunity that happened, but it was a surreal moment getting to meet a hero of mine."

"Telling those kids I knew him was something that had always bothered me," continued Johnson. "But when I told him, he said he was sorry that I had been bullied. Then, in a crowd of people that were there to honour him, He put his arm around me and said, 'Well, now you can tell them that we really do know each other.'"

"In a weird way, I felt a 'healing' had happened in that moment and everything had come full circle. Back then, I guess you could say he was my imaginary hero. But now, Dieter Brock is more of a 'real' hero to me because he cared."

Today, Dieter Brock lives a quiet life in Birmingham, Alabama, where some still believe he was the quarterback for the Winnipeg Jets. His back still bothers him and his knee occasionally flares up as reminders of what was. But the regret that continues to live inside the man is a constant nagging reminder of what could have been.

"Growing up in Brandon, it wasn't like my girlfriends gathered around the TV to watch CFL football," said Kathy KK Kennedy of Corus Entertainment. "Fortunately for me though, their older brothers and some of my family did! My introduction to Blue Bombers' ball began when the mighty Dieter Brock was quarterbacking," the CJOB and Power 97 host said. "The fact he could throw as well as he did, and have movie star looks? Well, I was hooked! And so began a love affair with this team, which continues to this day."

"Imagine years later, how giddy I was when I heard I would get a chance to meet and interview the man-the myth-the legend."

"So often a chance to meet an idol can be a disappointing experience. They don't live up to the vision you've created in your head. I'm happy to say, that did not happen with one Mr. Dieter Brock. He was just as knowledgeable and debonair as I had imagined...."

Today, Dieter follows the Winnipeg Blue Bombers than the Hamilton Tiger Cats or Los Angeles Rams with a combination of pride and regret. "I never should have left Winnipeg," he says now. "That was my team."

Off the field and away from the game, Brock had an impact that never hit the headlines. At the time, those moments were sometimes deceptive. They may have seemed mundane at the time, but those are the moments of greatness that some remember. And while fame may fade, greatness only grows as time pasts. It lives on as the stories are told and retold to generations that never witnessed The Birmingham Rifle on the field.

The opening line of this book was from CJOB's Greg Mackling where he said. "He pissed me off! How could he have done that?" Thirty-four years later, Greg Mackling, with his family had the opportunity to sit down with Brock and share some stories.

A few hours after leaving, Greg posted a comment of Facebook that is a fitting way to close out this book.

"To say tonight was one of those nights I could have never imagined as a kid; doesn't cover it," Mackling posted on Facebook. "Thank you so much for the hospitality and inviting us to spend an evening with some terrific people. The guests of honour Dieter and Jamie Brock were so kind to my boys... to see my boys give Jamie and Dieter a big good-bye hug was so heart-warming. What an incredible visit."

Greg's two sons had arrived with a football, hoping to get an autograph. The boys were too young to have witnessed anything Brock had done on the field, but they knew who they were meeting from their father's excitement and enthusiasm.

Sometimes we confuse the terms fame with greatness, but to be clear, there is a difference. Fame is what someone does for them self to gain wealth and status. In most cases fame is forgotten. Greatness, on the other hand is achieved by doing for others. Greatness is earned through perseverance, passion, humility and courage and can elevate someone to a fame that lasts more than a lifetime.

Dieter Brock is certainly a famous quarterback for what he achieved on the field, but his greatness will live on in the memories and moments he gave long after his statistics have faded.

As a national registered charity, the Never Alone Foundation has the flexibility to support many worthwhile agencies, projects and programs that aid in the fight against cancer. For more information or to make a donation to The Never Alone Foundation, please call 204-779-2441

The CFL Alumni Association fosters a lifelong relationship between the Canadian Football League and its alumni, and provides support to Alumni, to football in Canada and to other communities it serves.

The CFLAA unites former CFL players in support of: sport, youth and health related and charitable causes, former CFL players experiencing a medical challenge that creates a financial hardship; and promoting football in the community.

Dieter Brock Career

1967 Jones Valley High School 8-1-1 Placed third in State
1968 Jones Valley High School 4-5
1969 Auburn 4-1 Leading Freshman Passer SEC
1972 Jacksonville State 7-3
1973 Jacksonville State 7-2 Gulf South Conference MVP
1974 Senior Bowl First Jacksonville State Player Invited

Winnipeg Blue Bombers –Canadian Football League

	W/L	Att	Comp	Pct	Yrds	TD	Int
1974	0-1	27	12	44.4	176	0	2
1975	3-3-2	244	116	47.5	1911	11	9
1976	10-5	402	223	55.5	3101	17	18
1977	10-5	418	242	57.9	3063	23	19
1978	9-5	486	294	60.5	3755	23	18
1979	4-6	354	194	54.8	2383	15	12
1980	10-5	514	304	59.1	4252	28	12
1981	11-5	566	354	62.5	4796	32	15
1982	11-5	543	314	57.8	4294	28	15
1983	5-1	223	115	51.6	1892	10	9
Total	**73-41-2**	**3777**	**2168**	**57.4**	**29622**	**187**	**129**

Hamilton Tiger Cats – Canadian Football League

	W/L	Att	Comp	Pct	Yrds	TD	Int
1983	1-4-1	197	114	57.9	1241	8	6
1984	6-8-1	561	320	57.0	3966	15	23

Los Angeles Rams – National Football League

	W/L	Att	Comp	Pct	Yrds	TD	Int
1985	11-4	365	218	59.7	2658	16	13

Professional Totals

W/L	Att	Comp	Pct	Yrds	TD	Int
91-57-4	4900	2810	57.6	37488	226	171

- Quarterbacked 10 Playoff teams
  - 2 Western Finals
  - 2 Eastern Finals
  - 1 Grey Cup
  - 1 National Football
- First CFL Quarterback with 3 consecutive 4000 yard seasons
- First CFL Quarterback with 8 consecutive 3000 yard seasons
- 38 300 yard games
- 7 400 yard games
- 4 time CFL Touchdown Pass Leader
- 4 time CFL Pass Yard Leader
- 1978, 1982 Winnipeg Blue Bombers Most Outstanding Player
- 1980, 1981 Canadian Football League Most Outstanding Player
- 1985 National Football League All-Rookie
- 1985 Jacksonville State Hall of Fame
- 1990 Winnipeg Blue Bombers Hall of Fame
- 1992 Alabama Sports Hall of Fame
- 1995 Canadian Football League Hall of Fame
- 2016 Winnipeg Blue Bombers Ring of Honour

Made in the USA
Lexington, KY
23 September 2018